Summer Baby:

A Love Letter to Montserrat and the Journey to My Caribbean-American Identity

WENDELL C. WHITE

Wendell C. White

DEDICATION

To my mother, Violet Rose "Venus" Jeffers-Dazle; her mother, Jane Ann Lee-Jeffers; and her father, Joseph Richard Samuel Jeffers — the ones who loved me first.

Wendell C. White

Table of Contents

i Dreaming

I dream of Gages – an idyllic stretch of earth on the eastern Caribbean Island of Montserrat, bracketed by a hill and a mountain along the east road out of Plymouth.

A boy has incredible freedom in Gages to adventure on trails, fields, hills, creeks, and neighbors' yards until supper.

I miss the smells of ripe fruits in their season, fresh bread, tarts out of a neighbor's stone oven and the earthy smell of the livestock I would tend.

I dream of the sound of cars, vans, and trucks as they change gears at our corner on busy weekday mornings and evenings contrasted with the sound of silence on a Sunday, allowing the sound of distant laughter and shouts calling kids who had wandered too far from home. And the insects: Caribbean nights are alive with the sound of a million insects, their chorus lulling me to sleep.

I dream of lying on the squat concrete water tank, feeling the heat it had absorbed all day while gazing at distant stars -- wondering, pondering, and planning.

I dream of the people. Many of their faces burned into my memory while names float away like the conical blossoms from the cedars lining the ribbon of road. Sometimes while dreaming I will remember a name, but it's gone before I awake.

I dream of walking the ground with my sons, sharing stories and pointing to the places where my first memories were made. I imagine showing them my grandparents' house and explaining how the visible concrete structure envelops their original ten-by-fifteen-foot wood house, expanded in stages as finances allowed.

Then, I awake with a tear because that dream lies just beyond my reach.

Sharing Dreaming on Facebook sparked an outpouring of encouragement to continue writing, which planted the seed for Summer Baby. Join the Summer Baby Facebook group or email me at WendellWhiteWriter@gmail.com to share the memories my story stirs in you and to ask questions about the book.

Wendell C. White

ii Foreword

Summer Baby is a deeply personal memoir of my early years with my grandparents in Montserrat, West Indies, and my enduring connection to the island after reuniting with my mother in the United States eight years later, just before her marriage. It is a love letter to the island and the experiences that helped me bridge my Caribbean-American duality.

The experience of being cared for by grandparents or extended family transcends borders and cultures. Whether your parents left the Caribbean, the American South, Appalachia, Latin America, or Africa, the challenge of finding your place, of navigating your sense of belonging, remains a shared experience.

As you read this book, you may see reflections of your own family in these pages — the simple joys of summer days spent with cousins, aunts, uncles, and grandparents, the cultural practices adopted that at first felt unfamiliar, the freedom to explore, and the stories passed down through generations. The love, the laughter, and the life lessons from those who helped raise us are constants, no matter where we call home. This is a story for anyone who has ever known the feeling of being "home" in a place where your roots run deep, and your memories stretch wide.

iii Where is Montserrat?

Montserrat, a British Overseas Territory, is located in the Leeward Islands of the Caribbean. It lies about 1,200 miles southeast of Florida, 270 miles southeast of Puerto Rico, 27 miles southwest of Antigua, and 30 miles northwest of Guadeloupe.

Part of the Lesser Antilles, a volcanic arc forming the eastern edge of the Caribbean Sea, Montserrat is known as the "Emerald Isle of the Caribbean" for its rolling green hills and striking resemblance to Ireland's coastline. Montserrat is currently recognized for its Soufrière Hills Volcano, which roared back to life in 1995, eventually burying villages and the capital, Plymouth. The eruption created an evacuation zone and dramatically altered the lives of thousands of Montserratians.

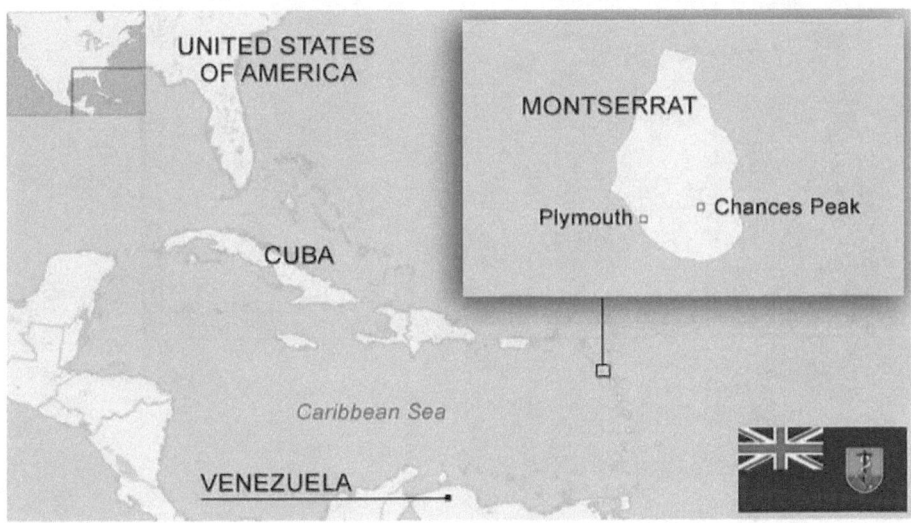

A detailed map showing the villages and Plymouth (Town) in the evacuated area, with a visual of the volcano's flows and a dotted line indicating the evacuated area. Both maps courtesy of the BBC

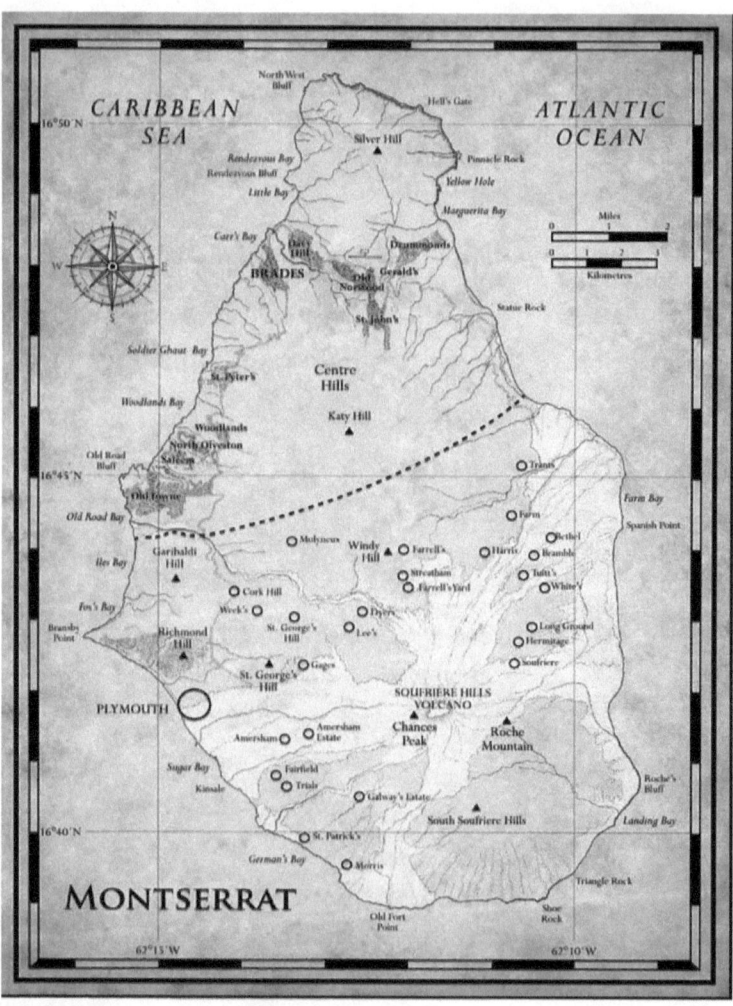

1 Summer Baby

I was just a baby in December 1970. A baby born in the heat of the prior New York City summer, now experiencing a shift. I couldn't have known what lay ahead, but maybe, even then, some part of me sensed gentle embraces waiting, the embraces of arms that would love me unconditionally, a place where I would belong, and a community that would love me as if my navel string had been buried under the roots of a local mango tree.

The story of how I arrived in Montserrat begins with my mother boarding an Eastern Airlines flight that December, from John F. Kennedy Airport (JFK) carrying her precious four-month-old boy and all the possessions a baby could have. We were headed to her parents and her island home. She carried gifts for her parents and friends, along with hope for a fresh start for her only child. Within a month, she would be back in the seeping cold of a New York City winter, working her 3 p.m. to 11 p.m. hospital shifts. She held the quiet ache of wondering why the man she had known since childhood now turned his back on sharing parenthood with her.

In later years, I would realize that his rejection, like biblical Joseph's, set steps in place that were meant for my good. It must have been a challenging time for my mother. Looking back, I can only imagine the hurt and second thoughts she must have endured. She would have to hear about her only child growing up from thousands of miles away. She missed my first steps, my first words, my first everything. I called her parents Mama and Dada and later called her mom. In a way, it may have felt like she was giving me up for an open adoption, but she knew it was for the best. Mama and Dada loved having me. It was like their new son had reawakened their hearts and their relationship.

Mom did everything she could to make up for her absence. She visited regularly and bought me everything a child could ever want. I imagine that she stocked up on all the spring and summer clothing sales to send to Montserrat, where the seasons hardly mattered. When other kids wore slippers, I always had closed-toed shoes that were overkill for the Caribbean climate.

Joseph Richard Samuel Jeffers, whom I affectionately called Dada, and others knew as Marse Joe, was fifty-four years old when I arrived. A six-foot-five-inch man with deep brown skin fitting tautly across his frame, he remained fit by swinging a hoe or fork every day as he took care of the crops he grew. He preferred shaving his salt and pepper beard and mustache with the cheap Bic razors that came six or twelve to a pack, wearing his mustache short of the corners of his upper lip. He always wore plain dress shirts over his white marinas (tank tops) and slacks, whether in the fields or at leisure. He smoked cigarettes, but not incessantly. I recall hearing him clear his lungs each morning. He drank alcohol, but never at home. Well known throughout the island, his name and reputation remain a memory among those old enough to have encountered him.

Born at the brink of World War I to a single mother with four children by four fathers, he received limited formal education but developed the working knowledge for all the botany, meteorology, and astronomy a farmer would need to know. He eventually passed that knowledge on to me, as well as any agricultural school could. Much of it I have forgotten because I wasn't required to depend on the land to make a living.

His father was a post-slavery estate overseer, who fathered dozens of children across fifty years. Dada was big on family. He knew, often pointed out and greeted his father's other children and their progeny as we moved about the island.

Mama, Jane Ann Lee-Jeffers, known as Sarah, Sally or Miss Sally, was fifty years old and barely five-foot-five inches when I arrived. Mama had spent some months with my mother before my birth and insisted she bring me *home* to Montserrat once she heard about my mother's post-birth challenges with housing, childcare and my father's support.

When I arrived, she had gained the plump frame all too typical of older Caribbean women. While most Caribbean women earned that frame from being metaphorically chained to working in a kitchen to prepare three hot meals daily for their family, Mama was thin until a lifesaving hysterectomy caused her to gain weight. She had started becoming chubby and developing the flabby triceps of that grandma who is always in charge of making holiday meals.

She too preferred standard clothes, no matter the task, so there were house dresses, town dresses, and church dresses. I do not think I ever saw either of them in shorts or a bathing suit. Mama was afraid of the water as she could not swim, and I faintly recall Dada bathing in the sea in his boxers.

They were not emotionally close or outwardly loving, but they shared jokes, stories, and by then, thirty years of marriage. They were much like the other couples of their age in our village, living after decades of marriage in a practical partnership rather than a romantic relationship.

She was religious, he was not. He brought the crops to her, and she sold them. When he earned money, he gave it to her. She took care of all the household finances, always careful to set aside her ten-percent tithe and an offering from any money that passed through her hands.

And so, this was my second beginning — a love story set in the folds of a rugged Caribbean Island both sides of my family had toiled on and called home for at least two hundred years, wrapped in the strength of the three people who loved me first.

2 The Scene

I spent my first four years close to home, often watching the world unfold from the veranda. The veranda was my playground – the only flat surface where I could ride my Big Wheel and tricycle – in an area surrounded by hilly ground and tight roadways without sidewalks.

Our house, like most in that part of Gages, was built into the base of St. George's Hill on the north side of the road. It was a sturdy, green-painted cement structure with a galvanized shingle roof and a prominent off-center front stairway. Wooden shutters framed the glass louvers – always ready to be fastened tight during storms. I loved the sound of rain on the galvanized panel roof. Its changing pitch at different storm intensities was a lullaby that cradled me to sleep. Even now, the sound brings me back to that safe, warm place, reminding me of the profound peace and love I felt as a child in Gages.

Being built into the hill, the house required twenty front steps to the veranda and front door. The lot's slope allowed for a full cellar and covered outdoor space under the veranda. A side door further up the hill on the left provided immediate access to a small dining room and our kitchen. The house's setback from the road allowed a large home garden to the right, stretching alongside the path from the road to the front stairs.

A majestic triad of mountain peaks, Gages Mountain, Chances Peak, and the then-dormant Soufriere Hills volcano, towering three-thousand-feet into the sky, greeted us at all times of the day. A Pan Am flight en route to New York City crashed into Chances Peak five years before my birth. Climbing the peak in search of the wreckage was a rite of passage for teenagers and young adults. Wet and slippery climbs to the top of the Soufriere to collect sulfur samples, smelling like rotten eggs, and marveling at the boiling streams was another coming-of-age tradition. I have personally made the climb up Soufriere but never up Chances Peak.

Between us and the mountains stretched a brief valley of agricultural fields and livestock pastures, nourished by the rich volcanic soil that made Gages the breadbasket of Montserrat. We could watch sheets of rain slowly creep across the dense green forests that blanketed the peaks, and moments later; the downpour would drench the valley below the mountains, before arriving at our house.

Living to the left of our veranda was Pupa George, an old, squat, light-skinned man with minimal wrinkles for his age. He lived in a simple one-room wooden house. His home sat closer to the road, just beside our garden and the handmade trellis for our christophene vine – known as cho cho in other parts of the English-speaking Caribbean and chayote in Latin America. To the right stood Tanty's house, Miss Trial to most, though her real name was Mary Riley. Her home was closer to the road as well, and together, our three houses formed a kind of misshapen triangle.

Tanty's niece and nephew, Edvira and Vincent, lived with her. Their mother worked abroad, leaving her children in Tanty's care as she tried to create a better future for all of them. Tanty, having lost part of one leg to diabetes, walked on crutches. Despite the crutches, she moved with surprising agility over the uneven ground outside her door. Edvira, the oldest of the two, was one of my earliest caregivers. Then a teenager, she took care of me as if I were her own child, her real-life babydoll. So much so that my Mama encouraged my mom to sponsor her to come to the United States when she was about nineteen years old. Vincent, the younger sibling, became one of my "big brothers" in the community. Our families shared a short, steep driveway ten yards from a blind corner, so someone had to stand watch on the other side of the road during busy times, to direct safe passage for drivers entering or exiting our driveway.

Tanty's and Pupa George's nightly conversations with my grandparents were a ritual each day. My grandparents would call out to them from our veranda, Tanty would respond from her living room window, and Pupa George would comment from his stoop. Each location was angled exactly right for them to exchange nightly conversations, often sparked by the evening news, weather, politics, or community gossip, which always ended with goodnights, like the closing of an episode of *The Waltons*.

The Cabeys, Peter, whom I always called Mr. Cabey, his wife "Boo," (I never knew her real name) and their sons Morris and Roy, lived to our left, looking from the street but to our right from our veranda. Mr. Cabey worked for the Montserrat Agricultural Department and was a star cricketer in his youth. Boo, a homemaker, was taller than Mr. Cabey. Morris, a mechanic, was one of the island's prominent bodybuilders at the time. Though shorter than Roy, he seemed larger than life to me as a child. I thought he towered over six feet tall. I was shocked to realize, when I met him as an adult years later, that at five feet eleven inches, I stood a full head taller than him. Roy worked as a tradesman in home construction. Roy inherited his height from Boo.

The Duberrys lived beyond the Cabeys, with their home closer to the road. Farmers like my grandparents, the Duberrys' twelve children migrated to England and Canada a decade before I was born. My mother's younger siblings followed a similar path of migration to England as part of the so-called Windrush Generation, named for the ship that brought most Caribbean immigrants to England at that time. The Windrush generation was part of a wave of workers from the then-current and former British colonies, who helped rebuild post-World War II Great Britain.

Mom secured her migration documents to Mother England, but she resisted going. She felt it too far away to return if her parents ever fell ill. Instead, she worked at the island's only hospital, waiting for her opportunity to immigrate to the United States. She got that opportunity and immigrated in 1965.

Joe Dry, as he was commonly known, and another of my "big brothers" in the community lived with the Duberrys. They adopted him after his parents separated. As is common in Caribbean culture, his real name was neither Joseph nor Joe Dry, but rather Desmond Corbett. The Duberrys also adopted Molly, perhaps five or six years older than me. Later, Junie, one of their grandchildren, also moved to be with them from Antigua. I did not learn that Mr. Duberry was my grandmother's first cousin until I was an adult. Perhaps that is why they did not mind me climbing their cashew tree or showing up at their house daily.

These neighbors defined the boundaries of my initial childhood wanderings. I could travel to their homes on the footpaths between our homes. My grandparents did not allow me on the narrow roads alone. Montserrat's winding and hilly roads held many corners and switchbacks. The section of the road between Gages and Lees was a relative straightaway in comparison, giving drivers a rare opportunity to get into fourth or even fifth gear, so many drivers indulged. Cars frequently sped by leaving no shared space for pedestrians, forcing them to leap onto embankments to avoid being hit. I lost two of my dogs to hit-and-run drivers on the road just in front of our house.

Beyond the initial fields just on the other side of the paved roadway lay a ghaut — a deep creek formed by water that had carved a fourteen-foot trench into the earth. Though the creek usually trickled, it roared after a rainstorm. It is reasonable to assume that an athlete with a good running start could clear the ghaut's narrower sections. However, no one I knew ever dared to try. The crossing points sloped down on either side, and if it had not rained recently, it was easy enough to find rocks or sandbars for a dry crossing.

A two-track dirt road ran parallel to the main paved east-west road, one hundred yards from the ghaut crossing. The dirt road met the main east-west road just beyond the eastern portion of Gages and led to Crosher (Krush-a) on its western end. Crosher was a small section of Gages – with primarily smaller all-wood homes. My grandparents first lived there before moving their small wood house along the main road and eventually building a concrete structure around it. I could still see the wooden slats and saplings used as studs in the original house in Mama's bedroom.

Though I did not know many people in Crosher, Mama often sent me to fetch eggs from a woman in the area. My maternal great-grandfather, John Zachary Lee, also lived there. Mama visited him regularly, bringing food, washing his clothes, and making sure he was well cared for.

Great-grandfather had returned to Montserrat in his old age after years of riotous living in Dominica. There was no father to greet him with a robe, a ring, or a feast. Instead, he lived out his days in one of the government-provided houses for the indigent. My great-grandmother, Ellenor Fergus-Lee, migrated to Dominica with him but had left him in Dominica and returned to Montserrat decades earlier. Great-grandmother, also known as Aunt Ellen, lived with Mama's sister, Elsie Lee-Smalle. Great-Grandmother had looked after Aunt Elsie's children as she worked across the Caribbean when they were younger. They resided across from my friend Dave Cassell's family in lower Gages, just beyond the Glenmore Estate, where the road began its descent toward Plymouth (town).

Mama and Dada 70s/80s. Courtesy of Marilyn Browne

3 Market Days

Dada expertly rotated planting and reaping so that there was a crop he and his small team could reap year around. As a younger man, he would "traffic" his produce, getting on ships and boats and selling directly to customers on other islands. Though those travels were behind him by the time I was born, his eyes still lit up when he talked about those days maximizing his profits.

By the time I arrived, he sold much of his products to the Montserrat Agricultural Department, which would sell crops internationally, aggregated from local farmers, in bags labeled Product of Montserrat. He maintained some direct customers, including hotels and the offshore American Medical school. Dada sold fresh milk to the Glendon Hospital, our island's only hospital, when calves were ready to wean. He milked every morning then stood in our driveway waiting to wave down the first driver he knew, to deliver his product to the hospital.

Mama sold the rest directly to customers at the Plymouth Market. The market was open several days a week, but Friday was her market day. She held the same spot near the market's left-side door for decades. In fact, she is in the background shot on an episode of Levar Burton's *Reading Rainbow* program. Levar brought his team to Montserrat to feature the book "My Little Island" by Frané Lessac.

Mama's sister, Mrs. Smalle, seated at her right hand, would help weigh and bag Mama's produce while selling the produce from her small home garden. The market, built below the front roadway grade, required buyers to take steps down into the "arena," where they would be met by a dozen voices clamoring for their attention. The spacing of the two doorways near the right and left corners of the building allowed for a broad middle section and then equal size sections to the left and right of each doorway. Mama's spot was in the shade of the roof lip of the market, just left of the left-side doorway. Sellers with less tenure competed for customers' attention as they came down the steps from uncovered tables near the roadway.

Market days were my favorite day of the week because I was able to help sell and experience the busyness of Plymouth once I became old enough. Mama would often leave without me because I could not get up in time or she did not have time to feed and clothe a little kid before her dawn departure. Dada would get me ready later in the morning and then flag down someone to take me to meet her.

The air changed the moment you entered the market. A mix of fresh fruits, vegetables of all varieties, fresh meat, and the salty sea breeze from the sea, one hundred yards behind us met your nostrils as you entered. The aggressive but friendly shouts of vendors, competing for the attention of customers, formed a din where individual voices barely registered. In my first few years, I would play with the scale weights and watch Mama and the other vendors. As I got older, I enjoyed weighing the produce, packaging it, or making an entire sale. I mean, who could resist a cute kid selling bright orange carrots?

By the time I was five or six years old, I was old enough to wander the market while Mama and her sister sold their products. The permanent vendor's stalls inside the market sold everything from pots and pans to lollipops. I remember buying toy cap guns, water guns, and candy cigarettes. Dada smoked, so I wanted to mimic him.

The butchers' stalls rimmed the rear right corner of the market. The butchers kept the unfortunate animals for slaughter in pens across a narrow street behind the market with the sand and sea beyond them. While I have seen many animals slaughtered for food, I was never early enough to watch slaughter in the market. The rhythmic chopping of cutlasses (machetes) partitioning the meat for sale alerted the market that the goriest part was complete.

Mama would finish just after midday, sometimes earlier. She would head next door to Ram's supermarket to buy essentials: flour, rice, sugar, crackers, cookies, saltfish (salted cod), and chicken parts imported from a southern US state that I distinctly remember came in white boxes as if they held donuts. Sugar was always brown and white; brown for us and white for baking and making lemonade for company.

She would leave her groceries with an employee or manager at Ram's and make a bank run and/or post office run. Her stop at the Royal Bank of Canada allowed me to get a hot dog or popcorn from the Wilson's snack shop across the street. Most rounds included a stop at Lett's, the ice cream parlor our neighbor Jaslyn eventually ran. I always chose soft-serve vanilla in a cone. We would head to the taxi-stand along the port after our final stop.

By the time I was ten or so, I would go to Wilson's shop and Lett's ice cream stand on my own while Mama was still in the market. I would additionally stop at the Bata shoe store or window shop for a toy I would later ask for as my Christmas gift.

Mama would have the taxi swing back to Ram's Supermarket to collect purchases she had left with the manager or other store employee. With stops completed, the taxi would make the steep climb from sea level to the Gages plateau.

Post Office in the foreground, War Memorial in the background, both along Marine Drive. Courtesy of Ivan Brown, Jr.

Early weekday at the market. Courtesy of Butch Pierce

Royal Bank of Canada in the foreground on the right,
across from Wilson's food shop. Her Majesty's Prison straight ahead.
Courtesy of Ivan Brown, Jr.

4 Preparation Day

Friday was Mama's market day, but it was also preparation day. As Seventh Day Adventists, we celebrated the Sabbath as a time of worship, rest, and refreshment, including attending church services on Saturdays. Friday was the day we prepared everything so that we could avoid unnecessary labor during the Sabbath. Adventists avoid formal work between Friday sunset and Saturday sunset. Those taking care of animals, healthcare workers, roles like law enforcement, firefighters and other first responders are examples of necessary exceptions. For kids at the time, it mostly meant you could not engage in raucous play or organized sports.

My maternal great-grandmother, Ellenor Fergus-Lee, was among the first converts when North American Adventist missionaries arrived in Montserrat in the early 1900s. Over the decades, Adventism had grown significantly on the island, amassing thousands of converts. The island had five churches spread across the parishes by the time I was a child. The Adventist community was socio-economically diverse, with prime ministers, business owners, professionals, and day laborers among its membership. This sense of belonging across social lines was one of the church's greatest strengths. Our neighbors, Tanty, and her household, as well as the Cabeys and Duberrys, were also Seventh Day Adventists.

Mama cooked the Sabbath meals and ironed our clothes when she returned from the Plymouth market. I had my own chores: putting away my toys, tidying the yard, and sweeping the ground beneath the bushes with a makeshift broom, made from coconut tree stems.

The distant sound of conch shells blowing might signal a pivot from the planned menu for Friday evening or Sabbath dinner to fish. Fishermen drove through the villages, their conch blasts summoning buyers to the roadside when they hadn't sold all their catch at the shore or when a particularly abundant haul coincided with a late return. With the truck bed loaded with metal tubs brimming with fish — usually garfish, jackfish and ballyhoo species — the fishermen or their helpers perched on the edges, ready to make a sale.

Infrequent customers had to hurry to the road and flag them down before the truck passed by. But at intersections and driveways with regular customers or multiple households, the fishermen lingered, blowing their conch shells longer and waiting just a little more patiently.

Dada typically handled the transaction, often securing a few extra fish for the same price. One of the fishermen might have been the son of a friend or shared some other connection — our small island was a web of familiar relationships. Dada also had a habit of preparing care packages from his crops: fresh vegetables bundled for friends and neighbors, handed off to their family members as they passed through. These quiet exchanges often bore fruit — literally and figuratively — in better deals on fish or occasional gifts of fresh meat when someone slaughtered a sheep or goat.

Shifting from the planned dinner to fresh fish required teamwork. Dada cleaned and prepared the catch, while Mama fried it to perfection — crisp and dry, just the way we all preferred. Dinner was always a delight, but the thought of leftover fish at lunch the next day made it even better.

We would bathe that evening, so it would be one less task to complete on Sabbath morning. Bathing in the evening also served a practical purpose — it's when the water was warmest. Like most of the households in the village at that time, we didn't have hot water. While many still used outdoor showers, we had an inside shower and bathroom, a result of one of several construction projects over the prior years. However, whether inside or outside, the water was just as cold before the sun's rays warmed the largely exposed galvanized pipes that ran from the main connection to each home.

As a child, I frequently bathed in a metal bathpan (bathtub) on a concrete slab just outside the kitchen. I got my water from the longest stretch of exposed galvanized pipe rather than using the shower inside, where the pipe ran through an area shaded by a mango tree. Outside, the water was warmer, and I didn't have to deal with the small frogs and lizards that often found their way into the bathroom, drawn by the dampness.

With preparations complete, we settled into our rest and worship. Sabbath began with our family's sunset welcome: singing hymns, reading scripture, and praying together. Afterward, we got a good night's rest, ready for an early departure to church the next morning

Mama and Elsie (sister) 60s/70s. Courtesy of Marilyn Browne.

5 Church Life

Church was the center of our spiritual life. We attended the Bethel Seventh Day Adventist church. The congregation worshipped in a building in Town Hill, an area above Kinsale, a seaside village south of Plymouth. I do not remember much about its interior, but the white-washed chapel stands out in my memory, especially the small courtyard surrounded by a low concrete fence. One of my earliest memories of church involves my "big brother," Joe (Desmond Corbett). I could not reach the pipe in the courtyard to drink water, so Joe cupped his hands under the stream and brought it down to me. His small act of kindness has remained with me for more than forty years.

Mama or Sister Jeffers, as she was known, had been a fixture in the Bethel Church since she was a young woman. Everyone knew her, but then, that was not unusual within the Adventist community. Like her consistency in Plymouth Market, she sat in the same seats or in the same general area week after week. Her seats were in the area where her Sabbath school group met, and she did not move to other seating after Sabbath School ended. After her Sabbath School ended, she would send one of my community big brothers to ensure my prompt transition to the sanctuary after the Children's Sabbath School finished.

Sabbath School started at 9:30 a.m., and the main service, known as the Divine Hour, started at 11 a.m. Sabbath School offered different content by age group with songs, tactile activities for the youngest children, and a review and robust discussion of the Bible lessons from the past week for adults. Sabbath School teachers followed quarter length lesson books the Adventist organization designed and printed.

We were usually back at home by 12:30 p.m., and that is when the rhythm of Sabbath rest truly began. Although Dada was not an Adventist at the time, he would share meals with us and observe the Sabbath's restful spirit. While he was not religious, he hummed along to the hymns we sang during morning and evening worship during the week and supported our religious observance.

Lunch was always special — chicken or fish with baked macaroni and cheese, potato salad, or rice and peas, alongside a fresh salad. Beef was a rarity in our home, but we occasionally had lamb or goat from our own flock or a gift from someone in the community. The afternoons were quiet, often spent napping or in nature. Dada preferred to go for long walks, and Mama gave me the important task of "keeping quiet" so as not to disturb her nap. Looking back, the goal of silence and stillness for a child was an impossible and unnecessary task for Sabbath-keeping. Children need activity.

Edvira used to take me as an infant to the Sabbath afternoon Adventist Youth Service (AYS), then called Missionary Volunteers (MV), until mom sponsored her to the United States. Her departure created a gap until I was independent enough to go with Roy and/or Joe. The afternoon service was by far my favorite part of the Sabbath. We sang from a more contemporary songbook, with guitar chords accompanying the songs. The service, full of skits, games, and interactive Bible study made the afternoon feel vibrant and lively in comparison to the morning services. We always closed the Sabbath at sunset, marking the end of our twenty-four hours of rest with song and a prayer.

As I approached my forties and now fifties, Sabbath afternoon naps have become my favorite part of the Sabbath too. While my own children have more freedom in how they spend their time than I did, their mission is similarly not to disturb my nap.

Church was not just about worship; it expanded my world. At first, I wasn't old enough or independent enough to fully take advantage of the activities and programs the church offered for preteens and youth. However, I fondly remember family-centered events, like church picnics at the beach and the annual New Year's picnic at the Amerindian Settlement in Trants. These gatherings created opportunities to build personal friendships that extended beyond our shared faith.

Through church, I met friends from other villages, including the Cannoniers (Wil, Delbert, and their sisters), the Tuitts (Arnold "Spoon," Orlyss, Horatio, and Craig), the Harrises (Walter, Myrna, and Steve), Terry, the Rogers, and many others. Adventism was, and still is, foundational to who I am and how I live my life.

A young Wendell. Courtesy of Marilyn Browne

6 School Days

Auntie Rita's Primary School in Groves was my first experience with education outside of church and home. The Groves complex, just outside of Plymouth on Montserrat's north-south road, primarily housed the island's Agricultural Department, with historical roots as a former estate/plantation. Though my memories of that time are faint, I remember our clothes, with my memory assisted by a class photo my grandparents kept for years on a shelf beneath their rarely used television. The picture was pure 1970s: children in bold, clashing colors and patterns that seemed both charming and outlandish by today's standards. We sat in two rows, wide-eyed, our hair meticulously styled, our clothing an eclectic mix of whatever our parents deemed appropriate. An Auntie Rita's classmate, Dee, recently reminded me that I had a penchant for bow ties and shirts with decorative ruffles, even on non-picture days. I thought my love for bow ties began later in life, but it was a habit I had embraced early on — an amusing glimpse into my personality taking shape at an early age.

Auntie Rita's was also the first place where I interacted with European and American children—children of expatriates, medical students, medical school instructors, and technical specialists who had come to work on the island. The exposure was new and surprising, as my little world, except for East Indian merchants and their families I saw in Plymouth, was otherwise racially homogeneous. We played side by side, unaware of the social complexities that adulthood would eventually reveal.

My next school was the Seventh-day Adventist School located farther along Montserrat's north-south road, just before it reached the village of Cork Hill. Our church sold the old Town Hill location and built a dual-purpose building in Delvins — dually used as a church and school. The building stood on a four-acre lot, its proximity to the road making it easily accessible for pickups and drop-offs. A narrow band of tropical rainforest flanked the ghaut (creek) that bordered the right and rear of the property. The sanctuary's platform sat at one end of the long, narrow building, while the Sabbath school rooms were at the other. It was a humble practical structure, built more for function than architectural flair.

The bathrooms were in an outbuilding with a broad lip of concrete connecting the entrances to the male and female bathrooms. The youngest kids would learn in the Sabbath School classrooms on school days. The upper grades gathered in clusters of desks around portable chalkboards, spaced throughout what would be the sanctuary on Sabbaths, after deacons placed folding chairs in neat rows on Friday afternoons.

School days in Delvin's had their rhythm. The east-west bus would sweep through the villages, picking up students from their driveways. I expect that a north-south bus did the same thing. Jaslyn, our neighbor, was a few years older and tasked with keeping an eye on me. We would sit under our regular tree for lunch, where she would lay out the meal Mama sent for me.

Without refrigeration at school, school lunch included picnic food: breads with cheese, butter, Vienna sausage, canned corned beef, sardines, and occasionally some fried or baked chicken. I had and still have a particular fondness for sliced cucumber and tomatoes with salt, so that often accompanied my meal. Mama sent imported fried chicken pieces, far larger than domestic chickens, that former classmates still kid me about.

School allowed me to meet Adventist kids from distant parts of Montserrat. Basil came from Dyers, just two villages east of Gages, while Andy was from Harris' Village, way out in the far eastern reaches of the island. I have lost track of Andy, but Basil went on to become a well-known figure on the island. He now hosts the morning show on ZJB, Montserrat's radio station, and serves as a charismatic event host and ambassador to the Montserrat diaspora.

Recess in Delvins offered as much freedom as life in Gages. We boys played games of cricket and football (soccer) behind the school. We used the concrete lip outside the bathroom as a surface for our homemade top battles and the ground nearby for shooting marbles. Our explorations often took us to the ghaut that ran from the right side to the back of the property. We dared each other to swing across rain-swelled ghauts after a storm, our hearts pounding with a mix of fear and exhilaration. We searched for iguanas sunning themselves in the treetops and watched tadpoles in nearby pools, marveling as they eventually transformed into frogs. And then there were the caterpillars — soft, colorful, and mysterious. We would trap them in glass jars, eagerly awaiting their metamorphosis into butterflies, then release them into the wild once they had completed their transformation.

Despite the school's lack of resources, there was a palpable sense of dedication among the teachers. They made up for what we lacked in materials with heart, and the parents — whether they were our own or the extended family who took care of us — sacrificed what they could to ensure we had the opportunity to learn. Looking back, it amazes me how much was achieved with so little. The teachers were our unsung heroes, fostering a love of learning in an environment that could easily have stifled it. God blessed the efforts of those teachers, as well as the parents, family, and church members who supported our school. Their commitment paid off. I consistently found myself at the top of my U.S. classes, thanks to the solid foundation my teachers in Delvins gave me.

7 Expanded Horizons

Starting school coincided with the start of more freedom, which came with new responsibilities. I would have to take our sheep and goats from our backyard pen to their grazing areas before school and bring them back home in the afternoon.

I started going with my grandfather to look after his handful of cows, typically staked in one of the unfarmed fields below Gages Mountain's tree line. I would do my best to help restake the ropes that held the cattle in new grazing areas and bring them water in a bucket or take them to drink from nearby water sources.

Within a couple of months, I could manage the work while he watched. I could independently manage a cow twenty times my weight by the time I was seven years old. They saw me as an extension of Dada and never tried to pull away from me. I remember daring my visiting older cousins to touch the huge animals on their neck or shoulder, while my seventy-five pounds and their familiarity with me held the cattle in place.

The Gages Estate, also known as Glenmore, sat behind a seven-foot stone wall on meticulously mowed grounds accented with flowering bushes. I often accompanied Joe to the estate, where his friend worked as the live-in caretaker for its foreign owners. Glenmore was one of the few remaining estate houses and outbuildings on the island from the slavery era.

Look closely at Montserrat's map, most of our towns and villages are the surnames of estate/plantation owners – Gages,' Lee's, Dyer's, Farrell's, Delvin's and White's - or topographical descriptions of the area. It's where the enslaved Africans worked and commonly the surnames we took upon emancipation. The Montserratians I share the White surname with are either genetically related or our ancestors worked on the same land.

Montserrat's history with the transatlantic slave trade began in the 1660s and persisted until Britain formally abolished slavery in its territories on August 1, 1834. Even then, the compulsory apprenticeship system effectively extended slavery for another four years, until August 1838. The unequal distribution of resources and lack of self-determination endured for well over a century after abolition.

The predominantly landless African population relied on sharecropping and land lease arrangements to eke out a living.

Without land ownership, they were excluded from voting and governance, perpetuating their marginalization. It wasn't until the late 1950s, amid a wave of independence movements and reform efforts across British Caribbean territories, that significant progress toward equal rights and self-governance began to take hold.

At Glenmore, I would watch Joe, and his friends play table tennis and other games in a walkout basement game room. No one ever talked about slavery in general and specifically our village's history as a plantation estate. It never dawned on me that this was the property where my enslaved ancestors' owners and/or overseers slept, and that most people in Gages were descendants of enslaved people who worked on Gages Estate lands.

Our neighbor Roy would take me on his Sunday afternoon trips to Foxes Bay. I learned the "head out of the water, legs dangling" swim style most people adopt when learning to swim in the ocean. While incredibly inefficient, I did not have to worry about drowning. Alternatively, I excelled at being able to hold my breath and swim underwater.

It was a decade later before I rebuilt my ocean-learned survival stroke into a freestyle stroke minimizing leg drag. Foxes Bay became a special place to me. I would explore the rocks at the far south end of the beach toward Bransby Point, where crashing waves created eddies holding crabs, moray eels, and small and occasionally sizable fish. A hot water pond, fed from an underground river, originating five miles away in the Soufriere Hills volcano, filled the depression behind the beach parking lot. Similar underground streams and rivers vented directly underwater into the Caribbean Sea. You would suddenly feel warmer water as you swam and played, identifying that you had just passed a venting volcano stream.

Large white egrets that traveled the island each day looking for insect treats from freshly plowed fields would return in V-formation at sundown to roost in the Bay's trees. It was amazing to watch them arrive – their numbers turned their sanctuary's trees white as they found roosts.

Foxes Bay had a simple outdoor shower with no privacy barrier, not much more than a three-foot wide by two-foot-high block of river stones and concrete with a garden faucet overhead. It was where we tried to wash away the black sand while trying to retain memories of a day at the bay. If it was the right time of year, you could throw stones or sticks to knock tamarind pods out of the seaside trees for a snack on the way home.

Permission to walk up the road in Gages broadened my network. Eltion, aka Joe, aka Bigwheel, and his brother Theodore, aka small Dadda, lived about five houses up and were in my age group. Their shared driveway yard offered a trifecta of attractions, watching work, food and friends.

I would hear a hammer hitting metal or the scorching sound of welding before arriving at their yard. Their uncle Morris had a makeshift body shop partially on the side of the road and into the driveway. There were not that many collisions in Montserrat, so he was more of a restoration specialist than a crash-and-dent man. He welded sheet metal to repair rusted-out floorboards, pounded out ancient dents, and worked magic with Bondo – the paste used in auto body repair –like joint compound for drywall. I watched him with intense curiosity, and looked at the torch flame I was not supposed to look at without eye protection.

Eltion and Theodore's grandmother, Miss Mono, owned a bakery bearing her name just up the street from my grandparents' house. The bakery sat at the top left corner of a rightward-sloping driveway, which it shared with three homes. Miss Mono and her daughter, Ms. Bella - Joe and Theodore's mother - sold freshly baked bread and treats baked in a stone oven in the back of the shop. They also stocked basic dried goods like flour, rice, and sugar.

There is nothing quite as satisfying as tearing into fresh bread slathered with butter, shared among hungry playmates hours after leaving home for the day. Adding soft cheese from a round tin can and a ripe pear - a green avocado common in the

Caribbean and Latin America, but not often found in supermarkets in the United States - picked from a neighbor's tree made it an even more indulgent treat.

James White Jr., or Biggie as we called him then, lived one house up, but their back door opened onto Joe's family's shared yard and driveway. While a couple of years older than us, James would frequently join in whatever we were up to. Biggie lived with his parents, Miss Hessey and Marse Sam "Hustler" White, along with about six other siblings. Alfred, John, and David, three of Biggie's older brothers, were Mama's nephews; sons Miss Hessey shared with her brother James Lee, who died at twenty-nine years old, when the boys were still young. I would continue a few houses east on the road, while hoping to catch a glimpse of Marse Daniel and Miss Nellie's attractive teenage daughters along the way.

Ms. Ella and Mr. Buffonge's house, by the last road along the main east-west road, would be the next stop. My grandfather used to tell me Mr. Buffonge and I were related, but I did not figure it out until doing my ancestry research five years ago. Mr. Edward Buffonge, aka Extra Strong, had several vocations, but in the time I knew him, he was primarily a butcher. He and Miss Ella lived at the last house before the road split, with the main east-west road continuing east and a spur that wound up to the top of St. George's hill, past Martha Rodney's house. Extra Strong was my grand uncle, my paternal grandmother's half-brother. The Buffonge story we were told is that Edward, and his brother Thomas, migrated from nearby Guadeloupe in the mid-1800s. As such, I am related to all Buffonges or Buffongs from Montserrat, one of the most common surnames in the diaspora.

Once at the end of houses along the road in Gages, I would walk fifty yards more along the main road to where the dirt road from Crosher intersected and made its terminal end. Optionally, I could walk back down the road to the nearest ghaut crossing, which might give me a second chance to see Marse Daniel and Miss Nellie's attractive teenage daughters. Once on the other side, I would "shout out," (say hello) to Jaslyn, before going to Marse John and Miss Barba Irish's house next door. They had a large flat dirt yard and a troop of mostly daughters. Their yard was a beehive of activity. With so many in the family, someone was always cooking, cleaning, handwashing, or putting clothes on the line to dry, often at the same time. Chickens pecked about the yard, and there could be a draft (checkers) game under a tree that I would watch intently. Dada had introduced me to checkers after I begged for a checker set I saw in a Plymouth shop's window for a Christmas gift. His impatience with my bad moves helped me to get good quickly. I recall one incident where he was so disappointed by my bad move while playing a kid my age that he angrily made me put the checkers board away. Before too long,

I regularly beat grown men on the larger draft board versions of checkers.

If the Irish's yard did not hold my attention, I would continue walking down the Crosher road parallel to the main road before, recrossing the ghaut (creek) at the nearest crossing to our house. With luck, I would come across ripe soursop from the tree that hung over the ghaut, guavas from the bushes I would pass, or a ripe tomato from the final field before I had to cross the two-lane main road to our house.

8 Outside

If a game show of that time asked where the Jeffers spent most of their time at home, the answer would unequivocally be their veranda. The veranda was where we entertained guests, cooled off, prepped vegetables for cooking, and watched the world go by.

Dada had a consistent spot at the left edge of the front door. Mama and I would trade off between a center seat against the house's wall and another close to the edge, pivoting from focusing on the road to looking back at the others. The gentle breezes made it an inviting spot to cool off after being in the fields or the small kitchen in the back corner of our house.

The veranda is where guests who dropped by in cars or my grandparents called from the road sat for a few minutes – usually offered a cool drink and a slice of freshly baked cake or plate tart during the Christmas season. It is where Nurse Marjorie Joseph would check their blood pressure as she did her community nursing rounds.

My family and our guests consumed incredible amounts of mangoes and sugarcane on that veranda. My grandparents could finish half a five-gallon bucket of mangoes in an afternoon. At the risk of disqualifying myself as a Caribbean-American, I confess that I do not like most mango varieties. I watched their aggressive consumption with a mix of admiration and repulsion. Sugarcane caused a vastly different reaction. We had the sweetest sugarcane stand in the village. Dada would peel and cut each joint into quarters before handing them to me and I ate them as fast as he could peel them.

In the morning, when Mama and Dada were busy, the veranda was my control center for boyish mischief. I would launch rocks at ground lizards from the safety of a raised perch and try to kill jack spanners (large orange wasps) that wandered under the veranda's ceiling. After success, I flicked them to the ground below, creating a feast for ants to take back to their nests. I had to go to school and church a few times with a swollen eye, evidence of the wasp battles I lost.

Car ownership was growing in Montserrat, but few people of my grandparent's generation owned cars in the seventies, and it seemed like ninety percent of the drivers were men. We walked to get anywhere in the village, between villages and even walked to and from town. Minibuses could be infrequent outside of the morning and evening rush hours, so you would start walking and hope that a minibus would pass you or a friend or a stranger would give you a ride.

Pickup truck drivers were especially generous at giving rides. They would pick up multiple walkers along the way. Tapping the cab roof or yelling "land me" was the common signal for them to stop to let you off. They would balance the clutch and gas pedal for just enough time to allow you to jump out of the truck bed and say thanks before they continued on their way. I did not start traveling this way until I was about twelve years old. Still, I was no stranger to the risks of traveling alone at an early age.

Airlines did not have an unaccompanied minor option back then, so I traveled between Montserrat and New York City with the oversight of someone my family knew or some compatriot they saw at the airport and asked to look out for me. This was a time when family could meet you at the gate, so I did not have to wander around New York's JFK airport as a four or five-year-old. The fear of losing my tickets was the scariest part of the journey. There were no easy reprints of tickets and boarding passes back then, so losing the card stock plane ticket was like losing cash. I feared losing my ticket as I transferred to a Montserrat-bound plane at V.C. Bird airport in Antigua during both the origin and return trips. I credit those early experiences with my comfort as an adult traveling anywhere in the world.

Airlines offered lower fares for kids twelve and under back then, so I made the trip to New York City to visit my mother frequently and reversed the trip once I moved to live with her in New York City.

9 Death with Different Stings

I returned home from school to an unusually empty house on a Thursday when I was six years old, in 1976. A freshly pressed dark suit was on my bed, with a note to be ready for someone to pick me up. Mama's father had died, and the funeral was that day. I recall attending his funeral at St. Anthony's Anglican Church at the far north end of Plymouth and his burial at the seaside cemetery across from the church. Both were on the road leading to Sturge Park, our island's major events venue. It was no big deal. I did not know him that well, and it was not unusual for an old man to die.

The death of my friend Theodore, aka Small Dada two years earlier, affected me entirely differently and continued to do so for decades after. In my young mind, children were not supposed to die. Theodore died in a freak accident in Kinsale. While working with his cousin Morris and learning the body shop trade, a dump truck lost its brakes at the top of a hill and ran through the body shop at the bottom of the hill, killing him in an instant.

I had nightmares and battled psychological pain for weeks. I avoided the funerals I could for at least the next four decades, until my wife challenged me to get through my reluctance and support the families impacted by death. I am embarrassed by the many funerals for individuals close to me that I found reasons to skip. It would have been good to have grief counseling for children back then, but nothing of its kind existed.

10 Christmas Season

The arrival of December brings an unmistakable excitement to the air in Montserrat. It's a season of anticipation – whether families are anticipating celebrating Christ, the Festival/Carnival season, the Christmas Barrel, or the joy of reconnecting with family who had traveled far – the island is energized.

Though Montserrat's weather doesn't shift dramatically, the nights and early mornings take on a cooler feel. It's just enough to bring out the sweaters, or for some, the thicker blankets sent from abroad, or the sweater, or the Members Only jacket they previously believed was sufficient for a mid-winter visit to family in the northern hemisphere.

The seas grow more boisterous, generating taller and more frequent waves crashing near the shore, making it harder for fishers to leave or land in their colorful wooden boats. The waves are strong enough to hold a young child or an adult who strayed too near the crash zone spinning underwater a few beats beyond comfort. An experience I am familiar with, but that is a story for another telling.

Seasonal decorations and blooming poinsettias are typically the first signs of the season. Those who hang light strings leave them on for a couple of hours between sunset and early bedtime. Dada would assemble a seven-foot artificial pine tree that just fit under the veranda roof. The tree's placement in the far-left corner of the veranda temporarily displaced his chair from his preferred position to watch the road, the valley, and the peaks beyond them. Out of place for the latitude, we were the only house I ever saw in Montserrat with a Christmas tree. I imagine my mom must have sent it to help me experience symbols of a northern hemisphere Christmas season.

Then came the coveted Christmas barrel, a symbol of love and sacrifice. These barrels were the lifeline of many Caribbean families, filled with dry goods, clothes, shoes, and other necessities that were either too expensive or hard to find on the island. The barrels would travel from large expatriate communities – in places like London, New York, Toronto, and Boston – with all senders ensuring that they dropped off their barrels with the shipper before the October deadline for holiday arrival. The flat charge, regardless of weight and favorable customs treatment provided relief from the year-round high cost to ship to Caribbean islands.

Mom kept a barrel in her small New York kitchen all year, gradually filling it with items on sale in preparation for the next shipment. When the barrel finally arrived, it would often contain heavy bags of flour, rice, sugar, and cans of sardines, salmon, or corned beef — along with clothes and shoes that I could grow into. The received barrel may have included a last-minute request for a cassette tape player or the replacement for a failing car starter. The barrel exchanged kitchens, coming from Mom, then finding a home in our small kitchen. Mama would capitalize on the extra surface for resting some of the cakes and coconut tarts she would bake for the season.

The season escalated with friendliness and frenzy. My grandparents, along with other neighbors, rushed to apply a fresh coat of paint to the inside and/or the outside of their already vibrantly painted homes. Families cleared yards and verandas of debris and clutter. Robust seasonal greetings from passersby and sharp car horn toots from passing drivers traveled on the breeze. Plymouth buzzed with added shoppers and visitors. Accidental reunions between old schoolmates may go something like this; 'Sylvester, boi a you dat? You get fat." This complimentary/non-complimentary introductory greeting would be followed by some storytelling on the street while the visitor's family waited impatiently or, if alone, over a few drinks at the Liquor Locker or another rum shop. Few gift exchanges occurred in our community; perhaps a single toy or new church clothes would be purchased for children.

Hearty greetings and well wishes reflected the spirit of the season more than gifts shared. Holiday visits often over cakes and coconut tarts, washed down by homemade sorrel, ginger beer, or a purchased Malt (Malta) or "sweet drink" (bottled soda) brought cheer to every face. Montserrat had a Coca Cola bottling plant with the traditional Coke along with various fruit flavors then. Christmas time called for buying one or more "sweet drink" crates for sharing.

News of new Calypso songs, pageants, calypso competitions, artist and steel band performances, plays, fetes, and cricket matches poured from any nearby radio. I was too young to participate, and we were Seventh Day Adventists, but even the most pious Adventist could hum the top new songs of the season, as they were ubiquitous from passing cars, minibuses, shops, or neighbors' radios. Interest in whose original song(s) and performance won the Calypso king and queen's final permeated all levels of society.

I looked forward to watching traveling masquerade troupes, made up of mostly men and boys who would dance to fife, guitar, banjo, and drum bands, who performed in suitably flat spaces. Trimmed by dozens of long, colorful strips, their costumes would gently counter their movements. A man in a bull costume called

John Bull sometimes accompanied the masqueraders and charged at frightened children. The group danced for tips but also accepted offered pastries and drinks. I have now seen similarly dressed figures across the African diaspora. I did not know it then, but the tradition appears deeply rooted in our African origins, with colonial influence in the added backing instruments.

The flat space at the top of the driveway in front of Ms. Mono Lee's bakery was a regular stop among otherwise sloping yards in our section of Gages. My grandfather would take me up the road to see the masqueraders. As I got older, I followed them for their next couple of stops.

Returning family members made this time extra special. They added energy to the seasonal activities and an economic boost for the island in large ways, and in the $5, $10 or $20 dollar bills they would surreptitiously share with family members and old friends. Returning islanders shared stories on streets, verandas, and around dinner tables of the big cities and how incomprehensibly cold northern winters were. The cost of travel and expected physical and cash gifts often factored into the low frequency of their return visits. Family members typically began arriving in mid-December but would be gone by the end of the first week of January, having departed with good memories, well wishes, tears, and hugs.

Mom often came during this season. She would join in the seasonal activities but mostly wanted to spend time with her parents and me. Her younger sister Josie and my four cousins arriving from Toronto for the same season made things extra special for me. Aunt Josie and Mom had remarkably similar features, except that Aunt Josie had inherited Dada's height. The four cousins, Brenda, Brian, Marilyn, and Charmaine, stair-stepped in age, each about two years apart. Brenda, the youngest, was a year older than me. I remember their slender height caught my attention. They each had a slight echo of Mama and Dada in their features.

Aunt Josie, the second oldest of Mama and Dada's children, immigrated to England when she was sixteen years old. Her younger brother Peter followed a year later to help stave off her loneliness. It is unfathomable in modern days to send sixteen-year-old children to a far-off continent by ship, without family to welcome them and with contact only by letters. But every family was doing it back then. Remissions from England were a major part of many Caribbean families' sustenance. Aunt Josie and her brood eventually moved from England to Toronto, Canada, when the children were still young.

Dada cherished his grandchildren, finding joy in introducing us to neighbors, associates, and friends with pride in his voice. News of our academic achievements often brought tears to his eyes, a quiet testament to how much they meant to him. He came from a generation where a child's extra hands were more valued than their education. Frequent periods of absence left him behind his classmates, who mocked his struggles. Feeling hopelessly behind, he stopped going to school by the third grade. He lived life as a highly functional illiterate. So much so that I didn't realize he couldn't read until my teenage years. He always made some excuse for why he needed you to read something for him, his missing glasses the most common excuse.

Yet, I believed my grandfather was one of the most intelligent men of his generation. His accomplishments while being functionally illiterate are still legendary to me. How does a man who cannot read, travel to England to work, navigate public transportation and survive for three winters before the freezing weather he endured chased him back to Montserrat? How does the same man run a farming operation, travel widely to sell his crops and run a small village shop without an innate intelligence?

Mama had reached eighth grade, allowing her an advantage in navigating the world beyond the fields Dada did not have.

The success of his grandchildren became Dada's own, the fulfillment of his potential realized through his progeny.

Looking back, I am not sure how we all managed to sleep in those three small rooms. The need for extra space, especially to host Christmas visitors, drove the decision to add a bedroom on the right side of the veranda, though it did cut into the stretch I had claimed as my tricycle and Big Wheel speedway.

Dada would kill a goat or sheep for these holiday visits. He could grab, kill, and hang a goat for skinning before the second bleat. He was handy with blades of every kind, from pocketknives to cutlasses (machetes). He was not the opponent you would want in a knife fight. I remember asking for and receiving my first pocketknife to be like him.

My cousins still tell the story of how I waited for dinner to tell them that the goat they played with yesterday was today's meal. They were horrified and could not finish it. To them, meat came from a supermarket. I experienced farm-to-table nutrition daily.

We consumed everything a goat or sheep had to offer. Dada would singe the severed animal's hair over a coal pot (imagine a clay Weber's grill) and then use the head and skin to make a pot of souse (meat stew of vegetables and various "extra" animal parts.) Spare parts that did not make it in the souse made it to our plates, typically served with rice. It was both practical, part of our Montserratian food culture, and, unknowingly to me then, our African food culture.

Mom would come alone, and there would always be a local suitor or two who would stop by the house to make their pitch. Mama's warning to Mom still echoes in my mind. She would tell her, "you going pick, pick, pick until you pick shit." Meaning that a woman approaching thirty needs to decide soon before all the good suitors are gone. But mom was not in a hurry; she had already been to the "amusement park," as fictional Rod Tidwell said to Tom Cruise's character in the movie *Jerry Maguire*. After all, she was a liberated woman, and it was the seventies.

Mom brought someone new with her that Christmas of 1977. His name was John, John Dazle, or more accurately, John Deazle, if the U.S. immigration department had not misspelled the family name on his United States immigration papers. He was originally from Antigua, born into a family of eleven children, with 15 years between the oldest and youngest's births. His parents had migrated from Barbuda, seeking better educational opportunities for their children.

The first thing I noticed about John was how much he talked — loud, fast, and often. In hindsight, it made sense. In a family that large, speaking up was the only way he could be heard. He stood about five foot eight inches. A wiry man befitting his carpentry vocation with light-colored skin like Pupa George and early balding.

We celebrated Christmas in Mom's house in Dagenham, a Plymouth suburb, just above Montserrat Technical College. She had it built for retirement after fewer than ten years in the U.S., a major accomplishment for a single woman. It had a modern open flow between the kitchen, dining area, and living room area with a washer/dryer and hot water heater, comforts we did not enjoy at Mama and Dada's house in Gages. Typically rented, it was vacant during that Christmas season, giving us a cozy place to gather.

But I was not cozy toward John. I was a brat to him. His presence triggered something in me — a deep resentment that I had carried for years about my father's absence. John also represented a threat, someone I thought might take my mother's attention, and worse, her money. My childhood mind imagined Mom had a chest of money and jewels common to children's books. I did not need a dad. Mom, Mama, Dada, and I were doing fine on our own.

To his credit, John took it all in stride. He realized he was just a target for my misplaced anger, and he was patient with me. Eventually, I recognized my behavior and apologized for being so rude. It did not make that Christmas perfect, but it helped.

That Christmas felt different from others, not just because of John, but because Dagenham was so close to Plymouth. From there, I could easily wander into town to watch the Christmas revelry. I remember climbing a small tree on Church Road near the library, watching the street bands on big trucks with crowds of people dancing, singing, and jumping in front and behind them. The street buzzed with energy, the rhythmic pulse of the Calypso and Soca bands filling the air. I decided at that moment that I wanted to play horns in a Calypso band one day – a decision still unfilled. The punch of the horns at the chorus captivated me. I also liked that they got to rest during songs, unlike the rhythm section — guitar, drums, and bass — who had to keep the groove going the entire time.

The Christmas season additionally included beauty pageants, Calypso artist competitions with divisions for children and adults, and men and women. Concerts and parties filled most nights for three continuous weeks. We left the magic of the season behind as the first week of January rolled in, carrying us back to the routines we knew too well.

Christmas Masquerade troop on the move. Courtesy of Sharon Robles

Cousins visit 1976. Rear 2ⁿᵈ from L, Charmaine, 2ⁿᵈ from R, Marilyn, Front: Wendell, Brenda and Brian. Courtesy of Marilyn Browne

11 Changing Places

I moved to the Bronx eight months after Mom and John's visit over the holidays in 1977. In some ways, it was like any other summer visit, but this time, I would not be going back to Mama and Dada before school started. I arrived in late July, about two weeks before my early August birthday.

We had no set plan for when I would move to the United States. My move happened after an emotional request that spring, a plea born from a desire for peace. Dada binge drank at unpredictable intervals. He would stagger home, then sit on the veranda and shout belligerently until he was tired enough to go to bed. He yelled about everyone who had wronged him, the in-laws he did not like and anything else that was on his mind. During one of these tirades, I broke down, crying to Mama that I wanted to live with my mother in New York.

In hindsight, his binge drinking and those outbursts were his way of coping, his own form of therapy. Dada did not fit the mold of an alcoholic — there was no daily drinking, no hidden bottles, or lingering scent of alcohol. He drank as if he were looking for a release, a place to let his burdens spill out, and when done, he would leave it all on the veranda. But if he had had access to real therapy, if he had had the opportunity for someone to hold those feelings with him, things would have been different. Mama's life and mine would have followed a different course, and I would have stayed in Montserrat a few years longer. Mom had an apartment in the St. Mary's Houses, 671 Westchester Avenue. They were rent-subsidized housing with your monthly payment on a sliding scale based on your income. Run by the New York City Housing Authority (NYCHA), most residents worked or were retirees. Two-parent families were not rare. Some high school graduates matriculated to college, typically one of the City of New York or State of New York college campuses. The Housing Authority did a decent job of maintenance. With two hundred and sixty-four households in each apartment building, it was impossible to know everyone. Five apartment buildings on the downtown (west) side of Westchester Avenue and one on the uptown (east) side of Westchester Avenue defined the community. Typical of NYCHA housing, you had swings and slides, basketball courts, and handball courts, with grass and concrete open space to toss a football, play stickball, and a bathroom by the recreational areas the NYCHA always chained shut to prevent them from being used for illicit drug and sexual activity.

They were not the worst of NYCHA Housing, but you still dealt with project life, elevators that were frequently out of service, an ongoing battle against cockroaches, and neighbors or visitors who found it convenient to urinate and defecate in the stairway.

We lived on the 18th floor in an apartment facing the street and the elevated Number 2 and Number 5 subway line. Our building was at its closest fifty feet from the structure holding the Jackson Avenue station. It is surprising how quickly your brain stops paying attention to a train's metallic screeching and the sound of conductors announcing the next stop. There were times when we struggled to hear a critical part of a television program, but otherwise, the sounds blended into the din of city life.

All around us were more projects, schools, grocery stores, convenience stores, dry cleaners, check cashing storefronts, takeout Chinese food restaurants, privately owned apartments, and bare lots where buildings once stood before landlords had them set ablaze for insurance settlement money. It was the ideal setup for a movie or videos depicting the declining South Bronx. I watched the filming of a portion of the music video for "The Message," the rap song by Grandmaster Flash and the Furious Five, from our window. Filmed just north of our apartment building on the other side of the elevated subway tracks, the song included the group's headliner Melle Mel rapping the pivotal lyric, "don't push me 'cause I'm close to the edge," which fully described the condition of many in the neighborhoods around us.

With the European immigrant and Jewish flight, the Bronx — particularly the South Bronx — became predominantly Black and Latino, with Puerto Ricans making up the largest Latino group. Dominicans and Cubans were part of the mix, but Puerto Ricans accounted for seventy percent of the Latinos and half the borough's total population. Most were poor or working-class, much like the other communities shaping the borough. Though generally of lighter skin color, Puerto Ricans are a wide range of skin tones, from pale to as dark as me. This was new to me; before coming to the Bronx, I had used skin tone as a quick way to group people.

We lived alongside Puerto Ricans, but my parents didn't have Puerto Rican friends, and I didn't have a close Latino friend until high school. While our parents may not have formed connections, young Black and Latino kids found common ground — especially in Hip-Hop. Together, we built Hip-Hop culture, which included rapping, DJ'ing, creating graffiti art, and breakdancing.

Rapper Fat Joe, of Puerto Rican and Cuban descent, grew up less than two miles from where we lived and later attended our common zone high school, just around the corner from my former elementary school. Of my generation, he often uses "Black slang," including the controversial N-word, treating it casually as just another noun to refer to himself and those in his circle, whether Black or Latino. For many in these communities — especially those without direct experience of the word's venomous history — it became a common term of camaraderie rather than a racial slur. To outsiders, seeing a light-complexioned Latino fluent in this slang and casually using the N-word might seem inappropriate. Yet, this dynamic underscores the shared bonds and unique relationship between Black and Latino communities during the birth of Hip-Hop culture.

Our neighborhood was safe by the standards of the 1970s South Bronx. I never experienced a criminal confrontation and didn't hear about neighbors being mugged or assaulted. Criminal confrontations were rare, though auto break-ins and the theft of car parts were common — driven largely by the area's high rates of heroin and alcohol addiction. At the time, heroin use was rampant in the South Bronx and Harlem, devastating families and fueling petty crimes as addiction tightened its grip on the community.

It was in that environment that I first heard the term eight-ball — an eighth of an ounce of cocaine, worth about $300 to $350 at the time. I was about ten years old, standing unnoticed at a neighborhood supermarket, listening to a conversation between the bagger and the cashier.

Both Latinos in their thirties, they spoke as though I wasn't there. The male bagger, beaming, recounted to the female cashier how the customer who had just left was a good friend who had recently gifted him an eight-ball for his birthday. Even then, I found it an odd thing to brag about. A mix of cultural, ethical, and anti-drug messaging had already shaped my belief that cocaine use wasn't something to celebrate. But powder cocaine, back then, was the drug of the rich and famous in Manhattan.

Looking back with less judgmental eyes, I can understand his excitement. For someone working in a neighborhood grocery store, receiving an eight-ball might have felt like a fleeting connection to power and wealth — a brief taste of the glamour associated with the drug in those days. It wasn't yet the crack epidemic that would devastate communities like ours in the 1980s. Back then, powder cocaine carried a veneer of exclusivity, glamorized in pop culture and associated with disco clubs, celebrities, and Wall Street excess. For someone like that bagger, it was probably less about the drug itself and more about the feeling of proximity to a world that seemed out of reach.

Most city kids develop a sixth sense early, which allows them to quickly spot potential trouble and divert their path. My sixth sense, Mama's prayers back in Montserrat, and being sufficiently acquainted with the potential neighborhood troublemakers allowed me safe passage to and from school and later across the city.

I had been to my mom's place many times before moving there in 1978. However, it was quickly apparent that a few weeks in the summer was far different from living there full-time. The first thing that hit me was the isolation and confinement. While I had been free to roam in Montserrat, I now spent a lot of time in the apartment and rarely left the front of the building and the kids' play areas on my own. There were no stops for me to make at familiar houses to stay for as little or as long as I wanted and no veranda from which to watch the world go by or battle my nemesis, the bright orange jack spanners (wasps).

The rest of the summer went quickly. I had a small birthday party where I met Diane, the daughter of one of Mom's friends and an elementary school classmate that fall. I accompanied Mom and John on their outings and watched hours of television on the black and white floor model my mom had. We had a TV in Montserrat, but it could only access signals for two channels on a mild weather day. Mama and Dada never turned it on unless there was some major regional news they wanted to see. A British Royal's visit to a neighboring island or cricket competition would qualify and be worth rotating the antenna until we had a decent picture. Mom and John did not watch it much either, both having not grown up with TV in the 1950s Caribbean. The TV existed for them as a barely necessary piece of furniture. Given their indifference, we did not get a color television until 1986, when the black and white television finally died.

Our stop on the elevated subway line. Courtesy of Kevin White

12 New York City School Days

I got my new school clothes a few weeks before school started. My new school's uniform included black slacks, white dress shirts, a tie and a green blazer with the school's name and insignia on the left breast. It read, "R.T. Hudson Elementary School" a Seventh Day Adventist School like the one I attended in Montserrat. Far more formal than the white polo shirt and khaki slack uniform I wore for school in Delvin's, this uniform branded you as an RT Hudson Elementary School student wherever a student traveled.

A controversy arose over which grade I would start in at RT Hudson. I had not attended a second-grade equivalent in Montserrat, but my age matched students entering RT Hudson's third grade. Thanks to advocacy from my former teachers in Montserrat and my mother's insistence, RT Hudson allowed me to start third grade with my age cohort.

John drove me to school for a couple of months and then I started walking on my own. I walked past the empty lots, remnants of the late 1970s widespread Bronx fires, and cut through other NYCHA housing. School day mornings and evenings no longer included having livestock to take care of before and after school.

RT Hudson Elementary School, at 1122 Forest Avenue, was a decades old brick building standing in what substituted for a residential neighborhood in the seventies South Bronx. Underfunded like my school in Montserrat, the school still saw its alumni continuously completing high school, matriculating to higher education, and entering distinguished careers.

All the houses on the school side of the block had been demolished as well as behind it, leaving empty lots of concrete and weeds. The brownstones opposite the school were surprisingly intact or at least physically intact on the exterior. However, you could tell by the torn or missing window coverings and the tenants shuffling to the corner store, that both the occupants and the building's interiors suffered from deferred maintenance. A large public elementary school took up the entire block behind us and Morris High School was around one corner.

RT Hudson's four-floor layout housed eight classrooms, a handful of administrative spaces, a music room in the basement and a one story added-on multi-function space on the far-left edge of the lot. The multi-function space alternatively functioned as a cafeteria, gym, and assembly space. The main building's layout was turned ninety degrees to the right from what it should have been. The centered entrance to the classrooms and offices was down the hall from the street-side front door.

I do not recall being anxious about starting third grade that fall as I should have been. It was a substantial change from school in Delvin's. My class had about twenty-five kids, twenty-four that I had never met and did not have much in common with. I doubted any of them had ever led a goat home, climbed a cashew tree, or even knew that cashew trees bore delicious fruit. Years later I discovered that while many of these kids were not Caribbean like I thought of myself then, they were the children and grandchildren of emigres like my parents and the Duberry kids – without the chance to live back home like I had. They had heard stories and visited a few weeks over their entire lives. They were the kids who waited impatiently as their dads caught up with old friends on the street or were shocked and scared by witnessing the slaughter of animals for food like my Canadian cousins. I was fundamentally different. I was Caribbean, Montserratian — or so I believed. But as I got older, I realized that while my lived experience in the Caribbean created a deep connection, in the U.S., my classmates and I weren't that different. We were children of immigrants trying to navigate the same balancing act between their family history and the world around them.

While at school, none of us revealed ourselves to be any different than other black and brown New Yorkers. But we were kids with parents or grandparents from somewhere else, trying desperately to not be "other." I tried to disguise my accent and word phrasing. We recited rap lyrics at lunchtime while maintaining the beat on the lunchroom table and in our off time or after school changed into the fashions of the Hip-Hop scene developing all around us. Boys played nerf football at recess and girls jumped double Dutch. During recess we shared a fenced backyard. Roaming the property's acreage or interacting with nature were no longer part of my recess agenda. We were in the concrete jungle.

My third-grade teacher, Ms. Nozil, was one of the younger teachers on staff. John drilled me on multiplication tables that year. Mastering multiplication would be my silver bullet to acing math for the next few years.

Mom and John did not want me to come home to an empty apartment, so initially I went home with John's niece (Thelma) and nephew (Anthony or Tony) to their home in the Castle Hill area of the Bronx. Their older brother Lloyd was already in high school. The two-family house included their parents, Joseph Martin, commonly called Martin, whose mother and sister lived less than a mile from Mama and Dada in Montserrat, Carmen, their mom, and John's older sister, Rosita, another sister, Sam, their youngest brother, the family's matriarch Mrs. Viola Deazle and a rotating number of family from Barbuda launching their lives in the U.S. Three other sisters and their families lived in separate houses on the same block ten minutes away. With other family members dropping by to see Ms. Deazle frequently, their multigenerational house was always buzzing with activity. John kept his boat and fishing supplies there and butchered deer in their garage after a successful hunt. Mom, John, and I visited as a family on weekends, and I stayed there many summer days with the other cousins. Summertime brought even more cousins and other visitors to the house. The always enterprising matriarch would sell ice pops to everyone passing through.

After I was a couple of years older, mom arranged with a widow in our building, Aunt Nell, a woman originally from Barbados, to keep me after school. I stopped going home with Tony and Thelma and instead returned to our building. Once in the building, I could go to the apartment but had to come right back to Aunt Nell's. I stayed with her from after school through the evening when John arrived.

Though walking was a more direct way home, I requested a New York City Transit bus pass from school. The bus pass allowed me more time with my Manhattan and Brooklyn bound friends who would be switching to the subway at 149th St and Third Avenue or a bus that crossed the Harlem River into Manhattan continuing a route to the Sugar Hill neighborhood in upper Harlem.

The bus rides totaled forty minutes from school to home, much longer than walking. But I was happy to have the time with my schoolmates. The bus would be filled with RT Hudson, Morris High School, the public elementary school kids, plus normal commuters. The high school students resisted lighting up a joint in view of the youngest kids. Exiting at Third Avenue, I would connect with the uptown Westchester Avenue bus for a few stops before it stopped across from our building.

The Watts, a family of Adventists living in the St. Mary's Housing building on the other side of the street attended RT Hudson Elementary School with me. Brian is a year or two older than me and Anita a year or two older than Brian. Cornell was several years younger, so he did not attend RT Hudson initially. We frequently commuted from school together, it felt safer that we were traveling as a small pack. Brian, Anita, and I later attended the same high school in Harlem, taking that same bus to the Sugar Hill neighborhood our RT Hudson Manhattan bound friends used to take home. Approximately ninety percent of kids from Adventist Churches attended Adventist Church Schools back then. Most of the kids had brothers, sisters, or cousins of various ages in school at the same time or who had graduated before. It made for a close-knit Adventist Youth community across New York City. It was through visiting other churches and interacting with RT Hudson and other Adventist School students that we got to know each other, and we dropped our masks a bit. Our parents were from the southern U.S., Jamaica, Trinidad, Barbados, Puerto Rico, the Dominican Republic, Costa Rica and elsewhere. Our parents and grandparents had not been so easily able to shed their accents nor cultural "quirks" as we were.

I successfully navigated the rest of my years, charming teachers whether they had reputations for being mean, moody, or merry. I got good grades, due to a mix of preparation, expectation, desire, and capacity. My grandfather was a major driving force for all of my academic achievements; I was determined to take advantage of every educational opportunity he did not get.

I was the salutatorian of our eighth-grade class, just .02 points behind my academic rival. We ran into each other a few years ago and shared a laugh about it. Or maybe she was laughing, and I was still masking forty-year-old pettiness.

Third or fourth grade RT Hudson school picture. Wendell C. White

13 John to Dad

At some point during my first year, John became Dad. He took care of me as if I were his own and his large family accepted me as well. He and my mom married a year after I had arrived, with me serving as the ring bearer. My brother, John Jr., was born that next year.

I cannot remember when I first started hearing about my biological father, but it was as early as I could understand language. Mama would frequently mention how my temperament, features and mannerisms were exactly like his. I resented these reminders. I resented him. I knew I was the child he chose not to father, and I used my resentment as fuel for achievement and demonstrating independent accomplishment.

While Dad cared for me as his own, he always left room for my biological father to play a role, should he choose to, but he never did. In doing so, he never fully addressed the closure I needed with my biological father. I longed for him to close the door, perhaps even adopt me and change my surname. When I asked him about it later in life, he explained that he didn't want to "disrespect" my father. A reasoning that, in hindsight, seemed far more noble than my father deserved.

Though educated as a Pharmacy Tech, Dad worked as a carpenter, primarily installing framing and drywall for residential and commercial interiors. However, hunting and fishing are his passions. I remember him taking me to hunt deer in the Catskill Mountains, during my first fall in New York City. He layered me in every warm garment I owned, stuffing my heavily socked feet into my blue rain boots. It was a comedy of me slipping and falling in the snow and speaking loudly, guaranteeing that every deer in the vicinity laughed at us as they snuck away. But he did not mind me ruining his chances. He laughed too.

Dad was born among the last three children in his father and mother's eleven child brood. They were a deeply religious family. His father worked hard to provide by farming, fishing, hunting, and sailing. His mother was a shrewd businessperson and achieved the highest returns for her farm goods.

She performed miracles by making food stretch for thirteen that should not have been enough for five. She bought fabric and sewed their clothes. She worked through each pregnancy, up until her children were ready to be born and would go right back to working after birth, putting the newest infant among their older siblings on a blanket in the shade of the field she was working.

They were never hungry or neglected in the traditional sense, but all of that providing did not leave his parents much time to be mom or dad to each child. No time for each child to have their own special moments, their own secrets, and jokes with their dad or mom. Instead, the older kids raised the younger kids. When at home, his father was only called on for worship, discipline, or meals. Dad's passion for hunting, fishing and seamanship comes from a desire to be just like his dad, the one he could watch with pride but had no time to spend with him individually, to teach him how to be a man like he was. He learned the skills to make his father proud from older brothers and distant observation.

So how does an Antiguan become enthralled with hunting? Dad's parents lived originally in Barbuda, moving to Antigua to provide better educational opportunities for their children. Unknown to me at the time, Barbuda had a rich hunting culture. Eurasian deer introduced hundreds of years ago for plantation owners and overseers to hunt still roamed the forest. Hunters tracked feral goats, sheep, and pigs with packs of dogs before dispatching the animal, often with ancient shotguns with as many homemade fixes as a Cuban Cadillac. Barbuda's lakes and estuaries were major stops on the North American waterfowl migration pathway, so Barbudans developed a waterfowl hunting culture as well. As for fishing, his father John Sr. was a professional fisher and farmer. With so many children, Dad's father did not have time to teach him any of these pursuits, so he learned from his older brothers.

He fished on the Long Island Sound almost every weekend, and some long summer days, after work as I was growing up. Nothing pleases him more than taking a kid or an inexperienced adult fishing. He would spend the entire day baiting hooks, clearing knotted reels, and helping the kids land fish. Initially he had a twelve-foot Jon boat he would tie down to his Chevrolet Impala. We would be off in a car full of his nephews, a couple of brothers and myself. That boat and its fifteen-horsepower engine held a ridiculous amount of us. We had a ton of fun in that boat, creating memories, and catching substantial numbers of fish he shared with his siblings. Dad later bought a seventeen-foot center console Boston Whaler fishing boat. It was the kind you had to trailer behind your vehicle with an outbound engine powerful enough for us to skip over waves instead of just riding slowly over them.

14 New York City Church Life

Dad didn't go to church regularly, but he would drop us off and pick us up. His parents converted to Adventism when he was a young adult, but he never developed a conviction or attachment.

Mom and I started attending the Bronx Temple of Seventh Day Adventists when I first arrived, a church in a converted bank building with too few voices to fill the vast space. We later began attending Smyrna Church, a Bronx Temple church plant located farther from home, near the Soundview area of the Bronx. The church met in a converted attached townhouse. Smyrna was our church home for several years – it was where we made and maintained strong relationships.

I occasionally attended the Bronx SDA Church where Tony's and Thelma's father Martin, their older brother Lloyd, and their grandmother Mrs. Viola Deazle attended, traveling by bus by myself from our apartment. Their mom Carmen, like John, was an adult living in England when her parents converted to

Adventism. She would attend when her nursing double-shifts had not drained the energy out of her by Friday evening.

Once I started driving, I would start the Sabbath at Smyrna SDA Church then end at Bronx SDA Church in the afternoon to meet up with the large group of kids my age that attended. In retrospect, Bronx SDA Church was unique with youth attendance. Many of my generation had parents with Adventist heritage who no longer attended church. Some of us had families who had moved to the edge of or outside New York City attended churches closer to their new homes, while their kids continuing a self-motivated trek back to the South-Bronx to attend Bronx SDA Church. The church had a vibrant youth community, held together with several teenagers who did not have to come to church.

We often stayed at church all day. Services were not as short as they were in Montserrat. Each church Department and constituency took their turns having their designated focus Sabbaths, providing lunch after church services that frequently ended at 2 p.m. or later. If lunch wasn't served, we could always find a kindly deaconess who would help us get fed from the canned vegetarian food store in the kitchen. Thus, we were able to stay fed while we enjoyed each other's company into the evening.

L to R: Warren, Bill, Wendell and Gilbert outside of Bronx SDA Church. Both photos courtesy of Andrew Brown.

Background: Kevin and Roger. Foreground L to R: Nigel, Bill and Tony.

15 Reverse Commuting

Once settled in the Bronx, I began reverse vacation commutes to Montserrat. I went every summer, several Christmases and even some Easter breaks. Back then, airlines had a discounted pricing model for children twelve and under, which financially allowed my frequent solo travel.

I tried to trick myself into believing I was still living in Montserrat and just attending school abroad. I would be sure to connect with my friends and neighbors. We would still do the same things, making slingshots out of saplings and rubber innertubes, making and flying kites, going to the ghaut (creek) to catch crayfish, picking red and black Jumbiebeads and whitish blue Groove seeds to make necklaces and wrist bracelets. Although I felt connected, the truth was becoming clearer: I was no longer local. It took me longer each time to fall back into the musical Montserratian accent. I was just a kid who visited from abroad like thousands of other kids in my generation who went to grandparents and aunties for the summer. There were new kids at school I did not know, inside jokes that I did not get, and even new neighbors in Gages I did not know. I still made my Friday rounds in town. I could take the minibuses back and forth by myself. Jaslyn had moved on from Lett's ice cream stand to the Harbor Court restaurant down the street, a block toward the harbor. I would always stop by and have a cheeseburger and fries.

My paternal grandmother, Dinah Buffonge-White had returned to Montserrat from living and working in New York by this point. I first met her when I lived in Montserrat full-time, and she visited from New York. She attended the same church as Mama, and they were close friends. She would often share candy or other treats with me at church. Their close relationship spanned back to before my mother and father were born. My then ten-year-old father would ride a donkey from Delvin's, around an ancient footpath at the base of St. George's Hill to Gages, to collect vegetables Mama would gift her family. Dinah insisted that I spend two weeks of my summer breaks at her home in Delvin's. Her house, built at the base of Garibaldi Hill, is just across the street and behind my old school. A pink house with a circular driveway – the blooming bushes and flowers along the driveway drawing visitors in both visually and olfactorily. The veranda at the top of the stairs ran the length of the house. The house had bedrooms on the left with a long combination living room and dining room in the middle with the kitchen, master bedroom, and another room on the right. I always stayed in the room in the back left corner. She was kind to me, but I never felt as comfortable with her as a child should feel with his grandmother. My father was still uninvolved. I had only met him once at that point, so perhaps our distance determined how close I could feel to his mother.

My Montserrat visits gradually shrank from entire summers to a month or a few weeks as I grew older. My reasons included wanting to spend more time fishing with Dad and cousins, and visiting my godmother in suburban New York City, and Mom's sister Josie, and my cousins in Canada.

I visited Montserrat twice during my high school years. In the summer of 1987, Dada rented a car for me. Dad had taught me to drive a stick shift in New York, but sitting in the right front seat, shifting with my left hand in a reverse gear pattern, and driving on the left side of the road required some mental adjustment before I could confidently hit the road.

Having the car opened the island to me. Though Montserrat is only five miles by seven miles, my previous travels had been limited to the route between Plymouth and Gages, with occasional passes through other villages along the east-west road to and from the airport.

The car gave me the freedom to explore the island's perimeter, visiting villages in the North and South that I had never seen before. I drove to visit friends to ensure we connected during my now shorter trips. I limed (hung out) at the roundabout in town on Saturday nights. I could easily get to full-court basketball games in Plymouth and drive to Foxes Bay as often as I wanted. Most importantly, I could take Mama and Dada on drives. For the brief time I was there, they felt the pride of their "son" being able to do something they never had, and they glimpsed the possibilities that having access to a car could open.

16 Rastafari

"Sing unto God, sing praises to his name: extol him that rideth upon the heavens by his name JAH, and rejoice before him." Psalm 68:4 - KJV

Rastafari emerged in 1930s Jamaica as both a spiritual calling and a defiant cultural identity for impoverished Afro-Jamaicans. Inspired by the Pan-African vision of Marcus Garvey, Rastafari grew as a belief system over the next four decades before spreading worldwide.

I do not know exactly when Rastafari first arrived in Montserrat, but it did not reach my attention until the late 1970s and early 1980s when young men in Gages and nearby villages began to convert. Their formerly neat afros transformed into traditional locks, maintained with meticulous washing and aloe vera from the island's prickly aloe plants. Rastas applied the biblical admonition that "cleanliness is next to godliness," to their entire body but especially to their hair, so hair washing became a ritual.

Tanty's nephew Vincent was the closest person to me, both physically and relationally, to convert. A soft spoken young dark-skinned man of average build in his twenties, searching for his place in the world, he abandoned his given name becoming Swaba, and leaving behind the Seventh-Day Adventist faith he had grown up in. By this time, Robert Nesta Marley's worldwide fame made him Rastafari's biggest ambassador. His influence spanned Jamaican politics, African freedom fighters, and both contented and disaffected youth of all hues and ethnicities. Perhaps he influenced Vincent as well.

At that age, I would not have known which questions to ask, but I remember my curiosity and sense of mystery around his new beliefs. I am sure he endured derision from the older generation, including my grandparents. I imagine my grandmother continually attempted to reconvert him back to Adventism.

I relocated to New York shortly after Vincent's conversion but would see and spend time with him on my frequent visits back to Montserrat. Our big brother, little brother relationship remained unchanged.

Though the deaths of Marley (1981) and their prophesied messiah Ethiopian Emperor Haile Selassie I (1975) slowed the growth of strict adherents, Rastafari culture continued to spread, bringing its I-tal diet, symbolic locks, sacramental use of ganja, and condemnation of Babylon — seen in corrupt systems and materialism — into global consciousness. Roots Reggae music played a significant role in the knowledge of and continuing conversions to Rastafari.

My next intimate contact with Rastafari came in the early eighties. Miss Ella had passed away, and her husband, my grand-uncle Edward Buffonge, went to live with his son, leaving Miss Ella's nephews, Fred, and his younger brother O'Neil, with the property. Fred — initially going by Tumba, who later settled on Ruta as his Rasta name, and O'Neil, originally known as Stone before becoming Jungle, were central figures in the Rastafari community in Gages and neighboring Lee's Village. Their property served as a hub for Reasoning sessions (worship), the exchange or sale of ganja, and entertainment — most notably, the infamous Rastateque, a live music event held on-site. Their property also offered a daily refuge for young Rastas, many of whom lived with family members who condemned the Rasta livity (lifestyle).

Three small wooden buildings stood in a staggered line from front to back on the left side of the property, with the right side open but shaded by tall breadfruit, mango, and coconut trees. The warm earthy aroma from roasting breadfruit and a pot of root vegetables bubbling on outdoor gas burners greeted visitors before they formally stepped onto the property. Fred, the taller and seemingly wiser of the brothers, had healthy brown skin, slightly darker than his brother. Both wore locks long enough to wind under their Rasta tams. Their yard became one of my favorite stops when I returned home. At the time, the irony of my granduncle having butchered hundreds of animals on the same property now occupied by devoted vegans was lost on me.

A small shop in the first building hugged Montserrat's east-west road. Crafts common to Caribbean tourist shops packed their shelves and floors — baskets, mats, hats, and other items, mostly woven from reeds and coconut husks. Running this shop was one of the ways the two brothers made a living. I have kept the vision of seeing O'Neil return to their property on the Crosher Road, walking alongside a reed-loaded donkey, in my mind for four decades. The brothers crafted many items themselves as well as enlisting area Rastas to produce items and sell to them at wholesale prices.

I watched these activities intently, holding brief conversations with Fred and O'Neil as they worked. Taxi drivers on their trips to and from the airport stopped with passengers, likely for a pre-negotiated fee. I would sometimes point out the quality of the items to the tourists and felt a small thrill when they made a sale. It really was quality work. I still own the woven basket I bought from them in the early 1990s, that over the years has served as towel storage, a college laundry basket, and currently a toy basket for my youngest son. Though the colored strands have faded, it shows remarkably slight wear.

Fred and O'Neil eventually took on empresses (common-law wives), Daphne one of the Irish family's daughters, I previously would hope to catch a glimpse of while passing their house. The other empress was from a village on the other side of St. George's Hill. Patriarchal at its foundation, Rastafari culture assigned empresses the roles of taking care of the children, washing clothes, preparing food, and helping with the business. With all her tasks, Daphne was too busy for me to have much more of a chance to look at her than when I would slow-walk past her parents' house in years past. The time spent at Fred and O'Neil's yard helped me develop a fondness for the Rasta livity (lifestyle).

While I reject Rastafarian theology around the divinity of Ethiopian Emperor Haile Selassie I, Rasta livity — living in harmony with nature, condemning materialism and capitalism, and following a vegan diet — still appeals to me. Roots Reggae is my music of choice, whether it is Bob Marley's limitless catalog, modern artists like Chronixx or Christafari (Christian-based reggae). Spending a Sabbath (Friday sunset to Saturday sunset) with Nyabingi Rastas (one of the twelve tribes or orders of

Rastafarian practice) in the hills outside Montego Bay, Jamaica is on my bucket list.

Nyabingi, the largest order of Rastafarians, are especially known for their unique drumming on traditional African animal skin drums with recitation and singing of Old Testament Hebrew Bible passages as part of bringing in the Sabbath and any reasoning (worship) session. It is deeply spiritual. And like every reggae enthusiast, I know that the proper response to an artist's call of "Jah" is "Rastafari." When the reggae band Morgan Heritage sings, "You don't have to dread (to be locked) to be Rasta," I receive that line as if they wrote it for me.

Rastafari has made a remarkable journey from marginalization and violent suppression to one of the dominant cultural influences on Caribbean and international society. Its influence is seen in language, music, and the normalization of I-tal (vegan) food and locks as a style embraced beyond Rasta circles. When founding Wailers member Peter Tosh sang "Legalize It" in 1975, I doubt he could have imagined the wide acceptance and commercialization of cannabis today.

I once asked Fred how he gained the skill to create such remarkable crafts seemingly overnight. He casually responded: "Jah give I vision." I thought he was just being coy. I mean, you do not learn those types of skills overnight. Then having never practiced literary writing, I began writing essays that became this book, I finally understood "Jah give I vision" too.

17 Roots and Culture

With my declining visits to Montserrat, I stayed connected with Caribbean culture through the food I ate, the music I listened to and burgeoning interest in the then dominant West Indies Cricket team, featuring star Antiguan batsman, Vivian Richards. Though our home menu included a few new dishes, much of the food Mom prepared mirrored the flavors of Montserrat, albeit missing some local specialties due to the lack of specific ingredients. Re-hydrated salted codfish for breakfast on Sundays, corned beef with white rice, ground provisions (boiled root vegetables), rice and green peas, stewed chicken and fried fish were all menu mainstays – sometimes washed down with homemade ginger beer or Sorrell. Mutton, goat meat and Caribbean fruit and vegetables were almost impossible to get in U.S. stores back then, so we adapted our palates to the American meats and fruits available, while longing for our return trips to indulge in whatever was in season.

The menu was much the same as the homes of John's large Antiguan family. While we kids developed a fondness for New York City pizza, hot dogs, and fast food, our parents rarely indulged in American street food cuisine. Even Jamaican beef patties were off limits for my parents to eat on the street. When we asked for "street" food we got the universal parent refrain, we have food at home. John was notorious for bringing a Tupperware container of home cooked food to eat between wedding ceremonies and receptions, so that it did not matter if he liked the food they served.

The members of the small New York City Montserratian community all knew each other, especially among Montserratian Seventh Day Adventists. It typically only took a few clarifying questions to make the connection. Conversations would go something like this,

Person 1: "You know Peter from north?"

Person 2: "Which Peter that? You mean the boy who used to dey (date) with that big-eyed girl?"

Person 1: "No man, Peter for Nen-Nen."

Person 2: "Oh yes, me know he. Why you never say that from the beginning? Sweet George is what we used to call him."

Beyond the food, music played a huge role in shaping our connection to Caribbean culture. By the late seventies, our local musical hero, the Mighty Arrow, had achieved Caribbean-wide fame and was on his way to worldwide fame. We also claimed Antiguan artists like Swallow and Short Shirt. Swallow's "Subway Jam Album" and Short Shirt's "Ghetto Vibes" album still take up auditory space in my brain.

Dad had a small sound system that he used for family birthdays, christenings, and other celebrations. He frequently bought the latest records to stay current with popular music, including reggae, Soca, Calypso, pop hits from artists like Michael Jackson and Cyndi Lauper, and slow jams by legends like Teddy Pendergrass and Marvin Gaye. He got them from Moodie's Records, located on the same block as his store. I had access to the sound system and often played those records at home.

Mrs. Deazle's birthday party, held every Thanksgiving weekend, was the social highlight of the family calendar. The guest list included every family member, her children's old classmates from Antigua, friends they had made elsewhere, co-workers, and, later, her grandchildren's friends.

The sisters cooked twelve or more hours per day in the three days before the party. At least four hundred people attended, with the party going on until the early morning hours. Worn out toddlers could be found sleeping on makeshift beds covered by jackets and coats. The annual event — significant as a reunion, connector, and teacher of Caribbean culture — was unlike anything I have experienced since they ended with Mrs. Deazle's move to Florida.

Family and friend functions were a major part of how I and people of my generation connected culturally. Caribana in Toronto and the Labor Day parade in Brooklyn were also major markers on our social and cultural calendars. The Brooklyn Labor Day parade as I knew it then secured the top Soca and Calypso bands to ride and play their hits live on huge trucks, just like they had in Montserrat. Masqueraders would be interspersed among the trucks, creating a sound break as well as showing off their colorful carnival costumes. Carnival revelers would follow their favorite trucks jumping and gyrating to the beats for the entire parade route or switching off to go with another band at some point in the spectacle. My favorite Labor Day Carnival Parade memory includes following Antiguan band Burning Flames during a time when one of their hits "Push Dem Down" created a mosh pit of pushing and shoving to song lyrics like "wet dem down" and "push dem down." Revelers carried buckets of water or buckets filled with confetti, as you would see in a clown show. You never knew what you were going to get. Burning Flames was a band for the young and uninhibited. Labor Day trucks had more traditional Calypso and Soca bands that you could jump and/or wave to without worrying about your wardrobe.

Given Canadians' orderly nature and wise public safety planning, Toronto Caribana was a much more organized Caribbean cultural celebration. The parade did not allow revelers watching from the side to jump into the action. The concerts and events often held on islands in Lake Ontario had appropriately roped off sections for each attendee category and the inability of quick off-island escape dissuaded potential troublemakers. Vendors appeared licensed and vetted by the Ontario government. One of the highlights of my Caribana years was selling records for Montserrat's Soca star Arrow in the crowd while he performed. John's youngest brother Sam had a relationship with Arrow through his Montserratian wife, so we met with Arrow and his team in the hotel before heading out to the venue.

Mom's sister Josie and her children lived in Mississauga, a Toronto suburb, so Caribana was a mini family reunion. While the rest of us were out once I was old enough, mom was able to spend hours with her sister laughing and reminiscing. The trips additionally facilitated time for me to spend time with my cousins, some who participated in Caribana events and others who did not.

Helping launch another islander into their new lives in Europe and North America is a common part of the Caribbean experience. Caribbean families are expected to sponsor relatives for U.S. immigration. Vouching for their character, providing a place to stay once they arrived and promising to provide the emigres with any needed financial support were all part of the commitment. Frequently, there would be a distant relative or child of my parents' friends who got their start by staying with us in the apartment. This meant I often gave up my bed for months at a time. Though inconvenient, their presence created a bit of a spark among us, because we got to introduce the wide-eyed newbies to New York City.

18 Dancehall Takeover

While I maintained my attachment to Soca and Calypso, by the mid-eighties, something else was getting my musical attention, Dancehall music. As New York City kids, we still listened to and enjoyed Rap and House music, but Reggae, Soca, and Calypso were what we retreated to on weekends – they were what our parents played to relax after busy workweeks, and what we heard at family gatherings.

Traditional Reggae, Calypso, and Soca navigated respectability politics, crafting messages that, after learning a few key words and listening closely, became accessible to a broader audience. Their risqué themes were skillfully cloaked in clever double entendres. Dancehall, however, made no such effort!

Dancehall abandoned the conscious anthems of Bob Marley and his contemporaries. It belonged to the then current generation of poor and working-class youth, focused less on peace, justice, and idealism, and more on immediate enjoyment and highlighting daily struggles. It sometimes depicted Jamaicans — and, more broadly, its Caribbean fans — in less admirable pursuits than the other genres. Perhaps because of this, middle- and upper-class Jamaicans looked down on it, and succeeded in banning much of it from Jamaican radio stations.

Our Caribbean parents ridiculed Dancehall, describing it as garbage music. Its journey mirrored that of its musical cousin, Rap music — and, for another generation, Rock and Roll — in their quests for acceptance, radio airplay, and TV exposure. Both genres clashed with the expectations of elders raised on the Black consciousness anthems of the 1960s and 1970s — songs that championed higher ideals and painted visions of a brighter future, often glossing over the harsher realities of daily life, and excluding primal desires.

For both Dancehall and Rap, achieving mainstream success required concessions to an older generation and the predominantly white, European-derived gatekeepers in the United States who controlled access to broader markets. Yet neither genre was willing to concede.

Unlike some of our parents or non-Caribbean peers, I didn't struggle to understand the lyrics. Jamaican patois was just another flavor of spoken English in the diverse mix of accents and dialects I'd grown up hearing in New York City's cultural salad bowl. The language's inaccessibility to outsiders only added to its appeal for me.

With the wealthy and cultural elitist limiting exposure on radio domestically, sound systems were how most Jamaicans on the island gained exposure to Dancehall. Jamaican sound systems began in 1950s. A Jamaican sound system was collective DJs/selectors, engineers and utility men who setup their turntables, mixers, huge speakers to play music in their communities. This was important in poor communities where many didn't have access to record players or radios. Eventually a party culture, food and drink vending developed around the sound system. Later some of the team began talking or chanting over the records. Sound systems evolved from someone sharing music in their community to packing up the equipment and traveling across the country, bringing the party with them.

Cassette tapes were how I first heard Dancehall. I do not remember how I got them, but I first started listening to cassette tapes with Jamaican artists like Josey Wales, Charlie Chaplin, Brigadier Jerry and Yellowman chanting (like freestyle rap) live on whatever rhythm the selector (DJ) put on. Some cassette tapes included one sound system, with the artists often tied to the same record label – their stable of artists passing around a single wired microphone between sips of beer and ganja. Another version of those cassettes were sound clashes where two different sound systems' artists battled for the crowd's approval to see who won.

Selectors competed for the audience's enthusiasm based on both the uniqueness of the track and the artist's flow. Audiences signaled their enthusiasm with a "forward," which could include loud shouts, holding lighters in the air, lighting small fires, banging on anything nearby, holding their gun shaped hands in the air and then mimicking gunfire, as celebratory gunfire was part of early Dancehall.

Dancehall Selector with DJs waiting their turn on the microphone.
Courtesy of Beth Lesser-Kingston, "Witness to Dancehall."

Dubplates — exclusive, recording masters of unreleased rhythms — gave selectors an edge over rivals and built buzz before the rhythm was widely available. The crowd's roar would rise as the artist freestyled or performed a hit over the selected "riddim," with a shout of "wheel" signaling the selector to restart the track just as the excitement peaked or the artist had exhausted their flow. It was a musical tease!

Some sound systems would try to increase their chances of winning by having special dubplate recordings that name-checked their sound system by bigger reggae artists or well-known international acts. These unique dubplates were like musical treasures and selectors guarded knowledge of their secret stash. Imagine suddenly hearing, "this is LL Cool J and when I am in Jamaica, I only get down with Volcano Sound." A dubplate could additionally include the guest artist singing, rapping, or chanting a couple lines boasting about the sound system and name dropping a few of their artists. It was the original Cameo! It was glorious and I could not get enough!

By the time Shabba Ranks burst onto the scene, my choices in clothes, music, and food were undeniably Jamaican. It was easy — most of my Caribbean friends from church and school were Jamaican. Jamaican music now dominated my music collection, Jamaican food shops were ubiquitous throughout New York City, and Jamaicans were the dominant cultural force within the

Caribbean diaspora. Of course, if someone asked, I'd say I was from Montserrat and do my best to describe where it was, in relation to more well-known places like Jamaica or Puerto Rico or Antigua.

I wore Clarks shoes, an iconic British brand that Jamaicans had adopted as their own. But not the popular styles like the Desert Trek, Desert Boot, or Wallabees. Fitting the rebelliousness of my music choices, I chose the least fashionable styles Clarks made. One of my favorite pairs featured pebbled leather and an unusually wide toe bed, stitched together with basic stitching that connected the top and bottom of the shoe about half an inch up from the sole. The soles mirrored the bumpiness of the pebbled leather, so you walked on the raised humps rather than the flat bottom. I had black and deep brown leather pairs. I especially loved how the footbed allowed my toes to stretch and flex as I roamed the streets or the dance floor. I adored those shoes, but I was apparently the only one who did — they had been discontinued when I needed a replacement. I'd pay good money for an untouched pair today, if someone found my size in the back of an abandoned Clark's warehouse.

My clothes similarly reflected my cultural shift, sometimes militant, other times flashy, depending on the occasion. I wore a red, gold, and green belt with the extra length hanging provocatively — when I wasn't around my parents. I could name every garrison (ghetto) mentioned in dancehall music, recognize every major sound system operator and music label. My brain created a map of Jamaica's geography, though I'd never been there. My accent would often shift to Jamaican patois in appropriate settings, the words and phrasing slipping in without any effort.

Many other Caribbean — and even non-Caribbean — young people were similarly drawn to the pull of Jamaican culture. I ran into my former Gages neighbor, Dave, in the Bronx during this time. He, too, had adopted the Dancehall "uniform." With his hair twisted, gold tooth caps, mesh tank top, and rings on multiple fingers, he looked ready for a dancehall reggae video shoot or a night out in Spanish Town, Jamaica.

I regularly attended parties with my Caribbean crew of about eight to ten guys from Bronx SDA Church back then, which foundationally included my cousin Tony, Gilbert, Andrew/Bill, Warren, and Kevin who I would later learn was a cousin. I don't remember how we were notified of these parties without cell phones or pagers, but we didn't miss many.

One mystery we still marvel at when the old crew gets together is why our parents allowed teenagers, as young as fifteen, to travel around the city on Saturday nights, by potentially dangerous public transportation, and return home on Sunday afternoons, with no idea where we were going or a way to reach us. I guess they considered us responsible kids – we were all still attending church, participating in church activities and neither drinking nor smoking.

A typical weekend would start with dressing in our suits to attend church. We'd pack our 'dancehall uniforms' in backpacks, stay all day until Adventist Youth Services in the evening, and then transform into our dancehall alter-egos before heading out to wherever one of us had heard a party was happening. Well, not all of us – though of Jamaican heritage, our friend Bill, preferred his Manhattan House music and Hip-Hop club attire, even when he joined us for Caribbean parties. Before heading out, we would fold our church clothes and place them neatly, along with our shoes, into our backpacks for the trip home on Sunday.

After exhausting ourselves dancing, we would crash at Kevin's house. Some of us would make it to Pathfinders, SDA scouting equivalent, or practice for the church sponsored track league the next morning. We would then wander home exhausted some time on Sunday afternoon, having to finish homework, while looking forward to the next time.

Our crew of guys spent at least thirty Saturday nights at Kevin's house during my high school years. Talking into the wee hours of the morning after parties and eating all his mom's eggs and bread on Sunday mornings, before she got fed up with us and banished us from her house. Kevin and I had been friends for eight years before his mom casually mentioned, "You know you all are cousins, right?" We did not know. We were sons of two brothers. While we had the same last name and our families were both from Montserrat, it was not a link we even thought about. Kevin's mom Ada divorced his father when he was an infant, and we were both distant from our fathers and their family. Ada's family was also from Montserrat and her dad was great friends with my grandparents. As with me, both sides of Kevin's family Including his parents were initially Seventh Day Adventists. Neither his mother nor father attended during his childhood. His maternal grandmother, who lived upstairs from him and his mother, strongly influenced church attendance during his middle school years, but by high school years, no one was making him. He found his way to church on public transportation, one of the Bronx SDA Church kids who attended church even though they didn't have to.

His maternal grandfather had retired to Montserrat and lived alone after living in the United States. He attended the same church as Mama. Mama and Dada would share produce with him, and he would responsively share dry goods and treats his children would mail from abroad.

We continued our Saturday night pattern for all my high school years and into my college years. Kevin's mom's banishment and the ability to get around the boroughs got much easier after a couple of us got cars. We developed a mutually beneficial relationship with a crew of girls from North Bronx SDA church. When we attended parties together, we sought to mingle and dance with others. We only danced with each other if the options were few and we made sure each of them partied and got home safely.

This is how I met Opal in the summer of 1988, the girl who would eight years later become my wife. While entering a party with Monique, one of the girls from the North Bronx all girls crew, introduced Opal as her cousin who just moved to the Bronx from Jamaica. I was polite in greeting her, while being anxious to move to the sounds from the speakers bracketing the dance floor.

Mom and Dad purchased a two-family house from an elderly Italian Immigrant widow in the spring of 1988, my high school senior year. While I was making the transition to college they were making the transition to a new neighborhood. The demographics of the Northeast Bronx were changing rapidly at the time. I worked in a door-to-door role for the 1990 census and would be surprised to encounter older Italian residents who had not learned English after more than fifty years in New York City or learned it with a mastery that they were willing to use with me. While some northeast Bronx neighborhoods maintained their Italian residents and character, much of the rest of the Northeast Bronx had changed or was rapidly changing into a Caribbean emigre neighborhood, like Crown Heights and other Caribbean sections of Brooklyn, New York. The move was great for me when I returned from college. Most of my party crew already lived in the area. And most of the parties we attended were now nearer. I would ride a cruiser bike I built out of spare parts to visit each of them on summer evenings.

White Plains Road, the main hub of the neighborhood, was lined with Jamaican takeout food shops, bakeries, money transfer businesses, Caribbean record stores, the footwear store where I bought my Clarks shoes at 219th Street, independent Caribbean grocers, furniture stores, and small discount department stores. The elevated section of the Number 2 train and the special Number 5 train run above White Plains Road creating easy access for the community to jobs in Manhattan and beyond. John and his brothers co-owned a small women's clothing shop on the uptown side of White Plains Road between 225th and 226th Street when I first arrived in New York City, so I was already familiar with the neighborhood. I spent many summers wandering nearby blocks and playing Space Invaders and Pac-Man video games in a convenience store across the street, between personally selling pantyhose, accessories, and the occasional dress, often to women who had just exited the 225th Street Subway station. Borrowing from comedian Charlie Murphy's hilarious retelling of an encounter with musician

Prince, who was remarkably good at basketball: If you think you are good at Space Invaders, challenge me, and make sure your people are there to see it.

Mom's apartment was much further south on the same Number 2 & 5 train line, so their home purchase and moving uptown was symbolic of a new status. But we did not live near the busyness of White Plains Road, we lived on the far east side of the Northeast Bronx, near Dyre Avenue, the last stop of the standard Number 5 train. The area was quieter than the blocks near White Plains Road and houses are built on slightly larger lots. Dad was able to keep his own boat and butcher deer in his own garage.

Group dinner. Rear: Troy, Warren and Wendell. Middle Row: Tony, Carl and Gilbert. Front Row: Kevin, Bill and Chris. Courtesy of Kevin White.

19 College Years

I began my first year at Duke University in Durham, North Carolina just weeks after meeting Opal. The first semester began smoothly — academics were manageable, and I connected with people who would become lifelong friends. Having gained twenty-five pounds between high school graduation and my arrival at Duke, I was determined to shed that weight and avoid the infamous freshman fifteen.

I dedicated three hours a day, five days a week, to the campus fitness center — rotating among the weight room, the balcony of Stairmasters and other cardio equipment, and the basketball courts. Many evenings, I fell asleep exhausted after dinner. The effort paid off; I lost two to four pounds each week and maintained solid grades throughout the semester.

While I continued to lose weight in my second semester, my academics took a sharp downturn. Spanish and Economics proved particularly challenging. I later learned that the

Economics class and that specific professor served the role of weeding out potential Economics majors. He even had a well-earned profane nickname. It was so rigorous that scoring sixty percent on a test could earn an A on the curve. Overwhelmed, I felt as hopelessly lost as Dada must have in third grade before giving up on school entirely. By late spring, I stopped attending those classes and braced myself for the consequences. Thankfully, my performance in other courses was strong enough for Duke to give me another chance.

Duke allowed me to return in the fall with a "prescription" for academic counseling. These full-time advisors worked closely with at-risk students, and their guidance transformed the rest of my college journey. My counselor taught me how to organize my schedule, develop productive study habits, and improve my writing skills. Together, we mapped out every thirty minutes of my day — allocating time for classes, post-class reviews, studying, projects, workouts, meals, and sleep.

This structured approach was revolutionary for me. In high school, academics had come easily; I could party on Saturday night, start a paper or begin studying for a test on Sunday afternoon, and still earn an A. Despite taking the highest-level classes my school offered, they weren't rigorous enough to prepare me for Duke. Many of my classmates had already encountered college-level material and instructors in high school, giving them a significant advantage and confidence. I, on the other hand, entered college with the same habits that had brought me success in high school — only to find they no longer worked. The struggle left me feeling isolated and caused me to question my ability to succeed at Duke.

Around the time I began academic counseling, I met two upperclassmen in the weight room. We frequented the gym at the same times, often spotting each other during heavy lifts or sharing a nod of acknowledgment from across the gym. Though our interactions were brief, they unknowingly became role models for me, showing me the discipline and dedication needed to thrive at Duke.

They couldn't have been more different: one, a reserved Black student from a bustling northeastern city; the other, a red-haired Southerner with a thick North Carolina mountain accent that could lead someone to underestimate his brilliance. They ate, showered then headed to the library after our gym sessions — staying until the library closed. I soon learned that it wasn't just the evenings, they would return at the library's open, leaving only for class or mealtimes. They treated school like a full-time job, devoting eight to twelve hours daily to studying. Watching them from afar kept me motivated to stay longer and work harder, even when I wanted to leave early. My academic counselor advised a daily hour of review, study, or preparation for each class on my schedule, but these two easily completed twice that, displaying the type of effort I would need to succeed.

The lessons I learned paid off. I became a B+ student for the rest of my college career, but the struggles of that second semester haunted my GPA. The discipline and structure I developed during that time continue to guide me today. Whenever life feels overwhelming, I return to the detailed scheduling and time management strategies I honed during those pivotal years.

I lost touch with the student from the North Carolina mountains, but I reconnected with the Black student on social media a few years ago. He serves as the Chief of Urology for a multi-state health system. I have no doubt that his college-era dedication fueled and continues to fuel his success.

I met David Suh during my sophomore year. He was a first-year student from St. Croix, U.S. Virgin Islands. We struck up a friendship, which led to us co-founding Duke University's Students of the Caribbean Association (SOCA). David's Caribbean story could be the plot of a movie. His Korean-American parents went to St. Croix for their honeymoon and decided to make it their permanent home.

David and I both felt the campus needed an organization to pull Caribbean and Caribbean American students into a community – an impulse we found over two dozen other students shared. It may have been David who came up with the organization's name – a name that both summed up our group and created a connection with one of the Caribbean's popular music genres.

SOCA provided fellowship for students directly from the Caribbean, those with Caribbean heritage, and anyone interested in the culture. SOCA fostered a sense of community and shared identity on campus. It connected both undergraduate and graduate students to the local Caribbean community. We partnered with Caribbean business owners in the Raleigh-Durham region, having them cater our events, hosting parties and other events at their venues and getting the word out about their existence. The food in the region was not as good as in cities we left behind in the northeast. We would excitedly share care packages of food and treats we brought back to campus after breaks and organized package delivery from parents, if one of us would be within twenty-five miles of our family when going home for the weekend. SOCA remains active on Duke University's campus thirty-four years later.

Though not an alcohol or beer drinker, influenced by my Adventist upbringing and watching Dada's alcohol induced vents, I developed a week-ending tradition of eating Caribbean food from a white styrofoam container – while sitting on my apartment porch or a nearby bench – sipping a Jamaican Red

Stripe beer. Though I didn't enjoy it, I found it tolerable — thanks to years of 'training' on non-alcoholic Malt[a] beverages since childhood! I recently joked to my brother and cousins that all the non-alcoholic beverages we grew up drinking in Caribbean culture are gateway drinks; Malt[a] a transition to a Guiness Stout and hops beverages, mauby, a tree bark-based beverage, to bush rum and sorrel with ginger beer to mixed drinks.

Family and Duke SOCA members at my campus apartment
L to R: Aleea, David, Wendell, Dad and Granny (Mrs. Deazle)

Hurricane Hugo, a Category 4 hurricane, devastated Montserrat in September of 1989, while I was a sophomore at Duke University. The slow-moving storm battered the island for twelve hours before continuing on its destructive path. Daybreak brought awareness of the scope of damage and the effort it would require to recover. Ninety percent of the houses suffered severe damage to total roof loss. The hurricane peeled roofs from their support walls, with some walls not being spared. The island had no power or running water for months. Residents carried water from the same ancient springs and creeks as their ancestors did. Bathing and washing clothes at creeks and rivers substituted for the conveniences islanders had come to take for granted.

Dad and a nine-year-old John, Jr traveled to Montserrat to help my grandparents recover. They were there for six or seven weeks before they were able to acquire supplies and reinstall the roof. I was starting sophomore year and did not join them.

While I had adopted Jamaican food, fashion, and music as my outward identity during high school and was not traveling to Montserrat as frequently, Montserrat was never far from my heart. I bent many ears talking about my homeland. So much so that it is the first thing people remember about me when I attend college reunions and homecomings. Through sharing my love and passion for Montserrat, someone told me there was another student at Duke from Montserrat.

What? I initially could not fathom that there were two of us attending Duke University. I quickly met her, and we struck up a friendship that we renewed in Montserrat every summer I visited. Nicole, the daughter of two of the island's most well-known businesspeople lived in the Foxes Bay community, a hilly Plymouth suburb overlooking the west coast of Montserrat and near my favorite beach. A preschool class picture Mama and Dada kept below the rarely used television confirmed that we had both attended the same preschool. We were both Auntie Rita's kids, reconnecting 15 years later!

I was by then old enough to lime (hang out) on Saturday evenings at the well-known roundabout in Plymouth, buying food and drinks from nearby takeout restaurants after whatever we ate for dinner had worn off. With my love for dancing, Nicole did not have to convince me to walk fifty feet from the roundabout to "La Cave," a dance club you had to step down into, and dance into the early morning hours. Ours was a surreal semi-annual connection on the island we both called home after having spent nine months attending college in a place so different and far away from Montserrat.

During one of those college summers, Nicole picked me up in her father's brand-new pearl colored Toyota 4-runner for a weekday evening visit at their house. Her mom was home, we met and exchanged greetings. She was just as flabbergasted as I had been that Nicole shared time at Auntie Rita's preschool, and we had now reunited at a college in North Carolina. It is likely that she offered me something to eat and drink and I accepted while the three of us talked in their open-concept kitchen and dining area.

Within an hour, Soca music came from a neighbor's house so loudly that we had to raise our voices to hear each other inside their concrete walled house. Nicole and her mom took it in stride. I finally asked who would dare to play music so loud in exclusive Foxes Bay. But it was not a recording, Alphonsus Cassell, better known as Arrow, internationally known for his hit "Hot, Hot, Hot" lived in their neighborhood. He was having band practice in his house, with all amplifiers turned up to 10 of 10. It was completely inconsiderate, but no one seemed bothered by the inconvenience. After all he was a national hero. The band played on through that entire evening visit.

I returned to Montserrat in 1990 and 1991 with a guest, my best friend and cousin Kevin White. These were his first times visiting the island. I had a rental car each time, allowing me to share parts of the island with him I had known since I was a toddler and ones I had just learned about once I began to drive. Both of us were heavily into lifting weights by this time, so Moose's gym, in Kinsale, a village south of Plymouth and along the sea, was a regular haunt during our trips.

"College days swiftly pass, imbued with memories fond" a lyric from my fraternal hymn, certainly captured my years at Duke. I finished college in the summer of 1992 and returned to New York City to start graduate school, continuing my journey of blending Caribbean and American cultures. Though school kept me busy, and a new group of friends invited me to social events, I still managed to revive our Saturday night partying traditions on occasion. By February 1994, I had graduated from Columbia University's School of Public Health, launched my career, and became engaged to Opal — all in the same year.

Kevin and I working out at Moose's seaside gym in Kinsale, Montserrat. Courtesy of Kevin White

20 When the Volcano Blows

By July 1995, I was in Michigan, three months from my wedding, when unsettling news rippled through the Montserrat diaspora: Soufrière Hills had awakened. At first, it was only distant tremors and then shockingly, ash clouds like talcum powder fell on Kinsale and other villages along the southwest coast. But within a year things would change. Volcanic ash frequently surged into the sky, shooting 30,000 feet high as the volcano began to reassert its presence. A fine, silvery dust fell over Montserrat and settled across islands as far away as Barbados, three hundred miles downwind. What began as occasional ash puffs in the air turned sinister as the volume of ash grew. Ash settled like feet of snow across New England rooftops, fields, and gardens, transforming formally clear pools into sooty basins and skies a brooding gray. Flights diverted their paths, and buildings shuddered under layers of ash, as heavy as sand. A fine film of ash settled inside homes as well. The film was impossible to defeat no matter how well or how often residents cleaned. Ash clouds large enough to block out the sun turned day driving into night driving in an instant. Drivers ineffectively used car wipers on the falling ash, before pulling over and accepting that the volcano was in charge.

The government acted early, announcing the first evacuations for villages closest to the hills soon after the first rumblings. My grandparents, who lived just across the valley from the Soufriere Hills volcano peak, were among the first ordered to leave. Schools and public buildings in the north of the island transformed overnight into shelters, filled with cots, curtains strung between families, and a dense hum of worry. Watching the news from my living room in Michigan, I could pick out familiar faces — neighbors, old classmates, mothers with children pressed close. They looked cramped and out of place, a community uprooted, now confined to rooms divided by little more than flimsy sheets.

In the two decades before Soufriere Hills reawakening, American artist Jimmy Buffett recorded the album "Volcano," at Montserrat's Air Studios. The title tune's catchy lyrics – *I don't know where I'm-a gonna go when the volcano blows* – then a fun poke at living on an island with a large volcano took on real significance. For some, the evacuations meant staying with friends or in guest rooms offered by generous neighbors; for others, it meant paying whatever was asked to rent a house or room, with some landlords using desperation to demand staggering rents.

My grandparents, Mama, and Dada, refused to go at first, insisting that home was safe. Afterall, they had lived in Gages all their lives, nothing was going to happen. They evaded the authorities by staying in during the days as patrols passed on the nearby road, and limiting nighttime lighting to the flickering wicks of ancient kerosene lanterns, which had seen use in the aftermath of a dozen hurricanes and tropical storms over the years. Their house became an island of resistance in an abandoned village. It took a tip from their daughter in Canada to local authorities and a visit from the police to finally get them to comply. Even then, they left reluctantly, packing lightly, certain they would return within weeks or months. Most families did the same, leaving pictures and valuables behind to an uncertain future.

They lived with an acquaintance in the north of the island for a few months, but space was tight, and even kindness came at a steep price. The rent, as high as for a whole house, quickly became unbearable. My parents urged them to come to New York City, also assuming it would be only for a few months to a year. But the volcano grew angrier. Quiet ash turned to raging rivers of superheated gas, rock, and mud. And at night, the mountain's eruptions, followed by fiery red streams of fire lit on the volcano's cone, were visible from neighboring Antigua. The volcano had commenced a seemingly unending cycle of building, collapsing, and rebuilding.

I visited Montserrat in 1997.[i] My now wife's friend was getting married in Antigua. Pyroclastic flows had claimed Montserrat's only airport and there were two ferries operating from Antigua in replacement for the fifteen-minute flights the airport previously allowed. The options were a four-hour trip on a cargo boat and a two-hour trip on a smaller passenger ferry. More than half of our population of twelve-thousand people had by then "temporarily" relocated to Antigua and other Caribbean islands, England, and the United States. The number would grow to more than two-thirds of the residents evacuating.

I left Antigua uncertain about what I would be facing and without a plan for lodging. I chose the larger cargo ship. It was my first time traveling to Montserrat by ship. Flying fish surfaced and glided for yards along the port and starboard sides as if escorting the vessel. I had only seen flying fish depicted on souvenirs of Barbados. Their gliding temporarily distracted me from the uneasiness of what I was getting into. With everyone I knew displaced, I did not know how to begin contacting anyone. Fortunately, I saw Mama's nephew Kenneth soon after docking.

He took me to where he was staying in a home belonging to a Montserratian off island who, like my mom, expected to retire to that home eventually.

Ash packed on the side of the roads reminiscent of plowed roads after a Canadian blizzard. A light but persistent coat of ash rested on every shelf, dishware, furniture, and walkway. Kenneth shared that he sent his family away to England and remained because he was two years away from earning his government pension. I recall watching one of the near daily ash clouds eject from the cone like cigar smoke and guessing on which way it would blow. I left within two days not sure what to make of what I had experienced but glad that I took the opportunity to visit during that surreal time.

Returning to Antigua on the smaller passenger ferry, I saw large suitcases awaiting loading suggesting that my fellow passengers were not just on a brief trip to Antigua but were instead escaping the island. Having spent a year of Sundays on Dad's boats by this time, I rarely got seasick, but I did on this trip. At the time I blamed it on being below deck, but looking back, my rush outside and regurgitation could have been my body's involuntary reaction to the swirl of emotions I held for the uncertain future of my beloved island.

Wendell C. White

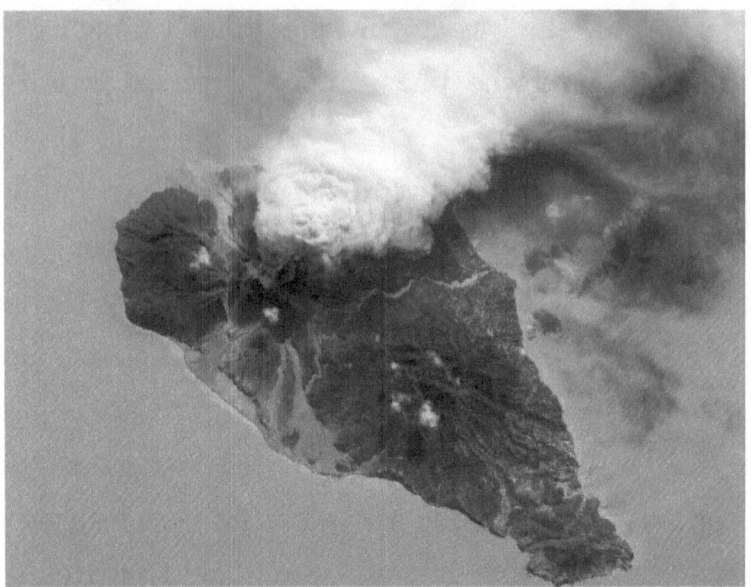

Volcanic activity photo from the International Space Station (ISS),
October 11, 2009.

21 Return Trips

I did not return to Montserrat until 2015, – eighteen years since my trip by ferry from Antigua.[ii] The 1997 dome collapse and pyroclastic flow into Plymouth ended any hope that life could ever be the same again. Residents tearfully watched the flows and fires erupt from their vantage point on Richmond Hill. Plymouth burned, just like the sportscaster Howard Cossell famously deadpanned about the Bronx during a summer 1977 New York Yankees broadcast, as flames filled the horizon behind him. Eruptions continued until 2010, with the last in 2013. Those of us in the diaspora remained riveted to any news out of the island. We bought and shared the latest pictures and videotapes of life on the island and volcano activity. An unfortunate consequence of the volcano was that more people had heard about the island on the news, and I did not have to explain where it was as much when I previously spoke longingly of home.

Mama and Dada had both passed by then, having never returned to their home and homeland. Dada died in 1999 from prostate cancer, the same killer that took his father and later one of his sons. He had converted to Adventism by the early 1990s, giving up smoking and drinking, and regularly attending church. Their New York City church family adopted them as their own grandparents and were active in visiting them when they could not attend. Dada apologized multiple times to Mama for all the pain he had caused her.

Soon after his arrival we learned that while in Montserrat he had taken it upon himself to get prostate cancer treatment in Antigua, rather than engage his children and travel to England, Canada, or the United States for treatment. Whether the physician botched the procedure, or the cancer just returned, the doctor Mom took him to in New York City soon after he arrived said it was too far gone and that he only had a few years to live. He lived out those years as actively and happily as he could. Though I lived in Michigan, I saw him multiple times per year and was in the house when he passed. The volcano evacuation allowed my brother to get to know them beyond their initial meeting in the weeks after Hurricane Hugo. In keeping with my role as their "son," Dada had conversations with me rather than my mother, aunts, and uncles about his final wishes for he and Mama before he died. He gave me the money to ensure no one would have to come out of their pocket to bury him or his wife. It was remarkable that he had saved enough money in U.S. currency, both for prostate surgery and their final expenses.

Mama passed away in 2007 from congestive heart failure. While Dada had always wished to live as long as possible, she had been ready to close her eyes and have them reopened by Jesus for at least twenty-five years. I was fortunate that she lived long enough to meet and hold my oldest son, who was just two years old when she passed. My grandfather, on the other hand, missed that chance. He shed tears of pride every time he saw me thriving as an adult. It brings me to tears now to imagine the joy he would have felt holding and teaching my sons, just as he once taught me.

Mama, and Dada with Aunt Josie in their later years in the US.
Courtesy of Marilyn Browne

Though volcanic activity became less frequent, Montserrat continued to lose population during the 2000s as more citizens accepted Britain's relocation offer. Then, when Soca legend Arrow and our national hero passed away from brain cancer in 2010 at the age of sixty, it felt as though the dream of reclaiming what Montserrat once was had died with him. But I couldn't accept Montserrat's death from three thousand miles away—I had to see its "corpse" for myself.

My wife and I traveled to Montserrat for our twentieth anniversary in 2015. My emotions were high. Once again, the journey would be by plane. By then, Montserrat had built a small airport 2,000 feet above sea level by flattening the top of a peak in the island's north. The plane was tiny, with an interior that bore the marks of decades of service. The close quarters made for fast friendships; we met everyone on the flight and greeted them warmly whenever we crossed paths later on the island. One young woman from Boston, Stanthia, became our travel companion for the rest of our trip and remains a friend today. The volcano had forced her family to flee Montserrat when she was a child. They initially settled in Jamaica before moving to suburban Boston, an area with a thriving Montserratian community.

As the nine-seater lifted from Antigua's airport, memories of prior trips rushed in. We landed after twenty minutes of the two propellor engines droning so loudly that we could barely hear each other. Our landing was uneventful. I remember stopping to kiss the ground, thankful that I had the opportunity to return home.

Though I was happy to be back, I couldn't shake the sadness for what we had lost. The far smaller population lives on a narrow strip of hilly land along the northwest coast of the island-fitting themselves around the Centre Hills' peaks.

How we met Stanthia! Wendell C. White.

Through binoculars, I was able to see Plymouth in the distance from abandoned Richmond Hill. I could identify my mother's house and the Bethel Seventh Day Adventist Church's permanent location, after leaving the dual-purpose building in Delvin's, across the road from it in Dagenham. I could see remnants of the Montserrat Technical College just below her house and the offshore U.S. Medical School in the distance.

Thanks to our guide's relationships with the National Volcano Observatory, we were granted access to restricted St. George's Hill. We entered the old roadway by unlocking and locking a gate behind us, near my old school. The blue Toyota 4X4 pickup climbed the hill and took us to look at prior tour highlights before taking us face-to-face with the volcano. We were also able to see the 18th century cannons trained at the harbor, which had been a tour stop in prior years, and the lone house on the harbor-facing side of the peak.

Selfie from a Centre Hills' peak, with Scriber Daley. Wendell C. White

The volcano's dome was unimaginably large. Soufriere Hills had pushed Gages Mountain and Chances Peak aside, making it difficult to identify where they had once been. The volcano and its flows filled the entire valley that once lay before us. Mama and Dada's house, along with most of the houses in upper Gages, were built on the opposite side of St. George's Hill we had accessed. While previously steep, the side of St. George's hill was sheared off by the volcano's explosiveness, leaving a cliff with an impossible angle to try to see remnants of Gages below.

Generations of feral livestock thrived in the evacuation zone. Residents leaving in the 1990s and 2000s had no market to sell them, so they released them. Cows, donkeys, and flocks of goats were visible on the ride up St. George's Hill and in the distance from Richmond Hill. They grazed among the concrete shells of buildings that once provided safety to the families who occupied them. Some house shells had fully grown trees growing out of their centers, reaching for the sky where there used to be a roof. Guavas and mangoes thrived unpicked along the road up to the hill's peak. Opal and our new friend Stanthia filled their impromptu t-shirt bags with dozens of guavas and mangoes on our climb up and down St. George's Hill.

Pyroclastic flow covering Gages and other villages. Wendell C. White

I was amazed people would find familiarity in my face as I traversed the island. They would stop and ask, who I belonged to, replying with confirmation after I told them, "Oh that tall man Jeffers, yes man me know you." My heart was full upon leaving, but unsatisfied because I could not travel to Gages, Plymouth or Dagenham. With no volcanic activity since 2013, the Montserrat Volcano Observatory (MVO) and the government started allowing guided daytime trips into Plymouth just five weeks after our September 2015 trip. I vowed to return, and both explore the remnants of Plymouth and hike to Gages if I could not take a four-by-four.

Volcano from the Montserrat Volcano Observatory. Wendell C. White

My next visit came in March of 2020 for the St. Patrick's Week Festival. Although a British colony for most of its colonial history, Montserrat's original colonists were Irish from nearby St. Kitts. Montserrat has the unique practice of being the only island in the Caribbean to recognize St. Patrick's Week both with somber remembrance and festivities like carnival at Christmas time. The somber celebrations commemorate a slave rebellion planned for St. Patrick's Day in 1768 when the Irish slave owning colonists would be too drunk from celebrations to resist. A female slave overheard the plot and told an Irishwoman who relayed it to the authorities. The colonists suppressed the rebellion, executed nine ringleaders, and sold another thirty to estates on other islands.

I traveled with my cousin Derrick, whose father and mother are first cousins, both sharing Dada's mother as their grandmother. I had hoped to share the island and enjoy the festival with him, but the world changed in March 2020. Just two days after our arrival, the government confirmed the first cases of Covid-19 on the island. The government canceled the festival and advised all visitors to leave. Despite the circumstances, we chose to stay for the ten days we had booked. We explored the island, took tours, and enjoyed small gatherings – officially sanctioned if we agreed to keep at a distance from each other – at local Rum Bars like Desert Storm in Salem, where old and new friends filled the evening with shouts and laughter. The government's shutdown included the Montserrat Volcano Observatory, and without their seismic forecasts, I had to cancel my plans to tour Plymouth and hike to Gages.

Derrick and I after landing on Rendezvous Beach by kayak.

My happy memories of life in Gages, Plymouth, and the other southern villages have sustained me through the sadness of loss since I last walked their soil in 1991. But my generation's memories alone can no longer suffice; they may even hinder progress if we hold too tightly to what once was.

Desert Storm rum bar in Salem, Montserrat. March 2020. W. White

Montserrat's future demands leaders who govern not from nostalgia, but with a vision for what is —and what could be. Our now unique blend of citizens holds the promise of a multilingual future, capable of forging economic connections across the Caribbean, the Americas, Europe, and Africa. With abundant sun, water, and geothermal resources, Montserrat could become a leader in sustainable energy and regional innovation. My hope is that the stories in *Summer Baby* remind us to value and preserve our roots while inspiring those on the island and in the diaspora to dream boldly and work together toward a brighter, more resilient future for all Montserratians.

22 Epilogue - A Different Death still Stings

In Chapter Nine, I wrote about the unexpected death of a childhood friend and how it shaped my life for decades—how it went unacknowledged and untreated, influencing decisions long into the future. The unexpected "death" of Gages and the southern region of Montserrat has affected me similarly. I've recognized the loss but never truly dealt with it. I was too busy with the demands of adulthood, especially as a husband and father. At some level, I didn't deal with it because it alternatively felt trivial and useless to try. After all, people endure much more dramatic trauma, and we've had no choice but to cope with nature's decades-long remodeling project while continuing to live our lives.

The Dreaming essay was born from emotions I could no longer keep bottled up—and perhaps never should have tried to. I suspect many of you reading this were drawn to the book because we share the same grief or can relate to it through a different loss. As Montserratians, our shared grief draws us closer, yet it often remains unspoken, untreated.

I see it in the photographs of brisk attendance at funerals of Montserratians scattered across the world. The frequency of those funerals has escalated, and my ability to recognize faces has diminished with time and age. I see it in the many Facebook groups created to unite us, in the online streaming rates for Radio Montserrat, and in the enthusiastic participation of off-island Montserratians in on-island politics. I see it in the high rates of return for Festival season in December, and for Green Week in March. I see it in the Montserratian gatherings you've created in your adopted cities. I see it in the vows of those resolutely determined never to return—whether because they want to preserve their memories intact or because they feel there is nothing left to go back to.

My life's journey has been one of transitions. I began by loving a place so deeply it shaped my identity. Then, I learned to balance that love while living in a foreign land—a place of my birth that never quite felt like home. And finally, I faced the ultimate heartbreak: seeing that place physically erased from the earth, and now, potentially from collective memory, by the same force of nature that brought it into existence.

This is the burden so many of us carry. If you are like me, I hope the experience of reading this book, the memories it evokes, and the sharing it inspires will ease your pain. But I also hope it helps you recognize that this grief—unresolved and often ignored—may still be holding you back or affecting those around you.

Let's continue to support each other in the ways we already do. But let's also take it a step further: seek individual or group therapy, grief counseling, or whatever helps you heal. As we approach thirty years since the volcano reemerged, the emotional impact still runs deep. I had been living in the United States for 17 years when the volcano erupted, and yet tears of grief flow as I write this. How much heavier must the burden be for those of you who literally fled the volcano's rage?

Our tears are not trivial. They remind us that a different Montserrat once existed—that our stories matter, that our small island home matters. And to truly thrive, we must care for ourselves as much as we care for the past and future of Montserrat.

Let this be a start. Meet me in the Summer Baby Facebook group or email me at WendellWhiteWriter@gmail.com

About the Author

Wendell White, a Central Virginia-based storyteller, shares a poignant tale in *Summer Baby*. Born in New York City, his heart belongs to Montserrat, West Indies.

Outside of writing, Wendell is a healthcare revenue cycle leader and Principal of HealthRev Advisors LLC. He has 25+ years of experience, driving over $150M in financial improvements, with improved patient access and operations for providers, to healthcare organizations. A Duke and Columbia University graduate, Wendell's passion for leadership and talent development defines his career. He cherishes time outdoors and traveling with his family.

---

[i] Versions printed prior to 2/13/2025 incorrectly state the year as 1996.
[ii] Versions printed prior to 2/13/2025 incorrectly state the years gap.